COLORS OF
MY DAYS

COLORS
OF
MY
DAYS

Donald X. Burt

THE LITURGICAL PRESS

Collegeville   Minnesota

Library of Congress Cataloging in Publication Data

Burt, Donald X
   Colors of my days.

   1. Spiritual life — Catholic authors.   I. Title.
BX2350.2.B867   248.4'82   80-23754
ISBN 0-8146-1198-2

Nihil obstat: Joseph C. Kremer, S.T.L., *Censor deputatus. Imprimatur:*
✝George H. Speltz, Bishop of St. Cloud, Minnesota, June 4, 1980.
   Copyright © 1980 by The Order of St. Benedict, Inc., Collegeville,
Minnesota 56321. Printed in the U.S.A.
   Cover design by Placid Stuckenschneider, O.S.B.

Contents

v

Introduction

I have a little friend who in her baby years had an odd interest in bathrooms. She would note with glee the various colors of the baths she personally visited, and she insisted that friends report back to her the shades of any room of rest that was forbidden to her. She proved the fact that we humans are born artists, surrounded by and consumed by color. We use colors to reflect our feelings on good days and bad days. We see red and feel blue and become green with envy. The Christian community recognized our need for color and assigned colors to the various periods of human life. There were the violet days of penance, the dancing pink of rejoicing, the green of quiet days, and glorious golden times of triumph. The life of Christianity is a life filled with color. So too our individual lives.

And thus it is that I can see my life as a succession of colored days. After the first tentative light of my early years, my days of waiting and being born and growing, there was a leveling off on the waters of a calm emerald sea. Days flowed into days easily during this quiet time. But then the wind seemed to shift and I came to the realization that I had grown older and that my days were becoming tinted with the rich mature shades of autumn. My life slowed even more and there was the beginning of a new waiting. At the very end my days dipped down from the plateau of ordinary times into the purpled shadows of death's valley.

The gray-white of waiting for birth, the placid green of ordinary days, the crimson-yellow of my autumn, the deep purpled blue of final days: these are the colors of my life. They are the varied colors of the robes of Jesus-God coming to be with me through all of my years. Perhaps these are the colors of your life too, for we are very much alike, my friend.

My life, like yours, is nothing more than a series of "todays." The center of my life is this "today" spent alone and quietly waiting for the setting sun. God *is* today if he is at all. I live only at this moment. My past times contain only what I was. My future is what I may be. I *am* today and though God is truly everywhere, he is present to me only here at the center of my today. Your life too can be nothing more than this: a succession of "todays." Some of them seem good. Some of them seem bad. None of my days are particularly world-shaking. I am neither pope nor president. I am just an ordinary man who has seen fifty years of mostly ordinary days. Even the length of these my days is not unusual. My days, all of them together, are less than a cough of the earth that supports me, less than a blink of the sun that warms me. My years are less than almost anything of note surrounding me.

And yet I need not be ashamed of my days. They may be ordinary when measured against the makers of history but they are unique. They cannot be duplicated by any king or conqueror. They are mine and, as such, are expressions of this "Donald" who, from all the limitless possibilities, was chosen consciously and loved into life by God. These days are my days and they happen because God wants them. God wants me.

On my good days I can easily believe that I am chosen by God and will live forever. On my bad days I don't really care. But to live forever I must first get through my today, whether it be good or bad. I must live today and not try to avoid it or cling to it. It may be helpful to speak about it. Perhaps in telling you the story of some of my days I will rediscover the love-prints of God walking through my life. Perhaps I will be encouraged to seek for him at this "here" during this "now," searching for him deep inside this special self, this Donald, that he loved into life and lives with today. It may be that today he is half-hiding like a child playing hide-and-seek, hiding just well enough to test the seriousness of the searcher, ready to leap out before me at my first sign of real interest.

I would like to speak to you, my friend, of my days. I know deep down that I am much like you even though on pompous days I try to blow myself up into something wonderful and on days of despair I feel like hiding in a thimble. We are very much alike. God has loved us both into life in our own unique ways but he gave us much the same baggage, shared needs and strengths. It is almost as though he were trying to tell us that we cannot face too many days alone. He knew that I needed sometimes to look into your eyes and see the joy and pain of being human. Looking into your life I can truly say: "There because of the grace of God go I. Are you in love? So am I! Are you in fear? So am I." Indeed, I must have all the same rooms in my life as you. Your folly and fears are mine. I share my humanness with you, and with Jesus.

Here now is the mystery: we share our good days and bad days with each other and also with Jesus. The days of our lives are his also. The colors of our days are colors that he has seen through eyes as human as ours. He gave us today. He loves us today. And most wonderful of all, he shares our today. So let us all talk about some of our days, the colors we see, the way we feel. Perhaps through our words we can see Jesus today. One thing is certain: "There is no use worrying about tomorrow. Today has troubles enough of its own" (Matt 6:33-34).

COLORS OF
MY DAYS

1   Days of Waiting

Gray is the color of my days as I wait for the coming of Jesus-God. The experience is like the very beginning of a New England November dawn. The cold mist is dark at first. There is no sky. There is no earth. There is only a still blackness. But then without warning there seems to be a lightening of the dark. There is no light yet, only a lightening. No cause is evident. There is no sun to hope for yet, much less to see. There is only this odd difference in the dark night as though something new waited quietly on the threshold of my perception. It is much too soon to tell whether the change is something outside me or is just a twitch in my straining eye. But something is happening to make my world brighter. I begin to hope. What the reality will be, in truth, remains to be seen. But this early grayness of the dark has awakened expectation. I realize happily that I am not simply *being* in unending night. I am *waiting*. How odd it is! I seem to have no present and yet I wait with anticipation for the future.

My days of waiting for Jesus-God are like that, beginning with a dark gray. They can come at any time. My life is a series of recurrent advents. Jesus comes and goes, or so it seems. Sometimes his goings are my fault. I think I am too big for him and throw him away like a toy of childhood, only to find that I have nothing to take his place. Then I wait in terror for him to come back because I suddenly realize that I lost the light through my own stupidity. I discover that without him I am blind and I cry out in sorrow, remembering what it was to see.

My need to wait can have less traumatic causes. As I grow Jesus must come again and again with messages suited to my growing

1

powers and his increased expectations. In all his comings I remain a child. Each time I am like a newborn having his first vision of un-wombed life. Dark confusion moves to gray and then to the white of sudden revelation. I seem born again and am overcome by a brilliant unfocussed whiteness. This white contains all the colors of my future but in an undefined way. My history lies hidden from the beginning in the expectations that Jesus has for me alone and in the grace he pro-vides to make his expectations possible for me. Whenever Jesus comes his birth is a surprise despite the long days of waiting. His reality always surpasses our dreams. Like children we are supremely happy without knowing exactly why.

When I was very young those shining white days after God's birth were wondrous days for me. I was not yet touched by guilt or fear of failure. Each day seemed friendly though not too clear. Knowing that Jesus had come, I could wait in confidence for the meaning to be ex-plained. I knew that I was loved. This was necessary for my hope. I needed first to know love before I could wait with hope for life to un-fold. Like a baby taking the first step, or like a toddler going to school for the first time, I was taking a chance on the unknown. I needed to know that someone cared enough to catch me if I stumbled. When Jesus was born to me I realized that it was he who loved me more than all. In his love I was able to enjoy the excitement of the unknown life before me. It was a unique time. Nothing was fixed. I had committed myself to no way of life. I had not yet declared my human loves. I had no fear of breaking promises because none had been made. I was free.

That freedom of Christ's first coming can never be repeated. When he comes to me now he finds me encumbered by history. I cannot repeat my day of first communion with him. Then I was just born, liv-ing in a world all bright and mostly bare. It was a world yet to be filled with the people and events that were to become my story. I cannot go back to those days. I should not try to. These later days of waiting have their own graces better fitted to this old child who has become somewhat gray himself. I still wait for Jesus to come but in a very dif-ferent way. Now I can reflect. I can think of his previous comings and goings. I can remember the day of his first birth when gray exploded into whiteness as the Son rose in my life. The gray before that first dawn was indeed somber, but never again will the darkness be so deep in my days of waiting. Now as I wait I can remember how fine it was when I saw the bright white brilliance of the Son for the very first time. And I can hope.

The Absence of God

The Christian time of Advent is a time of waiting. It is the season of God's absence. We call it a time of hope and are somewhat happy. But not completely, because our hope is a sign that we are not yet fulfilled. Hope is another name for the anxious future-leaning of present have-nots. The Christian Advent commemorates the God-longing of a people who have lost Eden. It reminds us of our individual advents when we wait in patient hope for an absent God.

The coldness of the northern Advent mornings, the silent frenzied thrust of naked trees against barely lightened skies, reminds me of my own barren days when my frozen heart struggles to rise and find its God. Sometimes my personal advents are worse than the season. There seems to be little promise of a new birth. God is absent. My life is dead.

Faith tells me that God is always with me, but experience seems to contradict. Experience testifies that if God is present always, he sometimes walks in silent steps. If God is always in my life, he sometimes is there quietly, like a new-made child sharing the life of a yet unknowing mother. Experience testifies that if God is always with me it is still easy to feel very much alone.

Why does this feeling of God's absence come? Who knows? Sometimes it happens when we reach out for new knowledge too brazenly. In learning more and more of the answers of the world we come to believe that we have all the answers. God seems childish. Our former faith seems no more than the false fruit of limited intelligence.

Or it may happen that we become disgusted with life. The story of reality begins and ends in absurdity. The world is not one in which God has become man. It is a world in which man tries to be God and fails. We become bitter with life and whatever God we had disappears in the acidity of our minds.

Or perhaps the disappearance of God can be explained as simply as this: we are torn apart by suffering and all we can manage is the cry: "Good God, if you exist why do I feel so bad!"

However it comes, the day of God's absence tears apart my life. Just as I still feel the pain of a newly extracted tooth, I ache for my missing God. I ache to believe in something. I ache to find someone who loves me enough and has power enough to say, "Let this affliction pass!"

Though I have lived a long time I am still a child. I still have the impatience and expectations of childhood. I expect that if God exists and truly loves me, everything should always be just fine. When events do not go according to my liking, I cry to be lifted from my damp crib and fondled by my loving God. I cannot stand to be left alone, not even for a second. I do not know how to live and to love in the darkness. I do not know how to wait for my loving God who seems to be temporarily away on other business.

Strange that I cannot be more trusting of a God whom I claim to love! Perhaps I really don't. Perhaps like a child I want him for myself, for the good things he gives me. Maybe that's why I get upset when he stops giving, when he waits quietly in my life for me to come to him.

Jesus, give me the patience to wait through the days of your absence. Let me remember your past goodness and be happy!

The Fears of Winter

There is no special season for unbelief any more than there is a special season for belief. But when I am waiting for God to come it always seems like winter, dark and threatening. My fears are those expressed in Eskimo lore at the approach of winter:

> We fear the cold and things we do not understand. But most of all we fear the deeds of the heedless ones among us (Loren Eiseley, "The Winter of Man," New York Times, January 16, 1972.)

When I wait for God to come I fear the lonely cold. I fear living my days with no one to love. I fear dying with no one to warm me with care.

When I wait for God I see the darkness in my mind and am afraid. I don't understand the universe around me. I don't understand those who are by my side. But most of all I don't understand myself. Oh, I may pretend to be wise and I laugh at the supposed superstitions of my ancestors, but I wear star-signs about my neck and am ready to worship any strange god who promises salvation.

When I wait for God I fear the heedless around me. I am overcome by the evil in war, the vile cruelties of the street, the hypocrisies of my race. I fear the heedless: my enemies, my friends, but above all myself.

When I wait for Jesus-God my winter fears can only be softened by the promise of the Son. God is! and no one ever lives alone. No one dies without the sun. God is! and thus we need not understand everything. Jesus cares for me even in my ignorance. God is! and thus the heedless need not be lost. Forgiveness is possible even for me.

In whatever season my winter wait for God occurs, I pray God I shall have hope by remembering other winters that have turned into spring. The winter world of God's absence is cold but not dead. Jesus does not seem to be with me just now, but he is coming. The Son will come with his warmth.

> Jesus, you don't seem to be here just now and I am cold. Send me some warmth to remind me that the Son will rise again for me and all my fears will go away.

Waiting for the Lord, Alone

John the Baptist is a model for me as I sit alone waiting for the Lord. He is an encouragement. He shows it is not wrong to wait for the Lord by myself. It is the way it is meant to be. Whitehead put this truth into words: "Religion is what the individual does with his own solitariness; if you are never solitary, you are never religious." I have talked about Jesus in community. I have sung about him with a crowd. But I must wait for him and find him alone.

This fact should not be distressing, though in truth there are some days when it is hard to accept the inevitability of my solitariness. There are days when I try desperately to break out of my cell of solitude. I want to be with people, to be surrounded by joyful noise, to find someone to whom I can reveal the mystery that is me. I want to share myself totally with someone else so that I will no longer be alone.

But it is not meant to be until I find the Lord. We humans may love each other deeply, but we can never know each other completely. Young parents express regret that they have so little time to be alone together. But even if they had the time they would discover that each has a cell of solitude that cannot be given away. Ultimately this cell of solitude means that I can only be alone with myself. It was this cell of solitude that determined that I must be born alone. It was this cell of solitude that determined that I experience love alone. It is this cell of solitude that determines that I shall die alone. And it must be through this cell of solitude that I wait for Jesus to come to me.

John the Baptist seemed to know this. The gospel presents him to us as a happy man. He accepted his solitude. He rejoiced in it. He danced in the desert alone because he sensed that his solitude was not a curse but a call to listen quietly for the whisper of God pointing out the Savior. And John's mission was fulfilled when, standing alone in a vast crowd, he pointed to that one person who could surpass his solitary splendor: Jesus-God walking by himself among the throngs.

John is a comfort to me as I wait for each new birth of Jesus in my solitary life. In my waiting I am separated from the rest of humankind, but I am not separated from God. My waiting for Jesus-God does not mean that he is not with me now. His coming to me will not be in the form of a lengthy trip from some foreign land. Rather it will be a gradual revelation of his hidden presence in my solitary life. He is with me now as I wait for him in solitude. Someday he will be revealed just as one day Mary held in her arms the infant son who for nine months lay hidden deep within her quiet, solitary self.

Jesus was with the Baptist in the desert and John danced to the tune that God sang to him alone.

Jesus, you see me as I am in all my uniqueness. Your words say that you redeemed me in that aloneness. You love me alone. You call me to be alone together with you for eternity. Give me the courage to

wait for you alone so that I may soon hear your voice
whispering in the midst of my solitude.

Being Still and Waiting with the Lord

On days of waiting we are sometimes encouraged by remembering
the message of Advent: "He is coming!" It does not strike us just how
strange that assertion is. God is everywhere (we are told) and hence
what sense is there in crying "He is coming!" But then, he is not the one
who insists that he is coming. We are, and our cry is at least understandable. Such is the turmoil of our lives that our lives seem nothing
more than a series of comings and goings: our coming as a child (only
faintly remembered); the going of our youth (with difficulty accepted);
the final coming of death (fearfully anticipated). Coming and going
seem to constitute the fabric of our lives and consequently we are
consoled by promises of a Savior who is coming. The promise of a God
who is coming gives us hope. We say: "One thing I know for sure: he is
not here now! Otherwise how can I explain my frustrated dreams of
finding the fullness of love, of realizing my ambitions, of escaping
fear?"

    And thus it is that present discontent prompts my scurrying about,
my coming and going. I do not feel saved all that much here and now
and thus I am ever moving on in hopes of finding the Savior on some
new day in some new town. I grimly come and go, arrive and leave, trying to capture the peace which always seems to be just out of reach. I
never dream of the possibility that the Savior is right here in the midst
of my days of waiting. I can't imagine in my distress that Jesus-God is
not coming at all, that he is right here at this very moment. I can't
believe that there is no need for me to speed frantically through the
static universe because I and Jesus are at the center of things right
now. All I need to do is to sit back with Jesus and watch the beauty of
the universe swirl past. I can't believe that I need not try desperately
to go home. I am home. The great revelation of my life will not be the
discovery of some foreign God in some distant kingdom. It will be that
God has lived with me through my days of waiting, that through all my
comings and goings he was here and we shared life. The great awaken-

ing for me will be the final firm realization that Jesus is not coming. He lives, right here and now.

There are times in the process of life that I suspect this truth. For instance, when I experience love I can sense the presence of Jesus' love. In the moment of love it sometimes seems that time stops and dances about the lovers in wonder at such perfect giving. When we sit quietly with someone we love it is easy to believe that God is near. It is easy to be patient, to sit quietly and wait to see there with us the God who has made such great human love possible.

The awareness of God's presence can also come when we are alone. For instance, when I sit by the sea on a perfect morning my rushing seems to stop and suddenly I am at peace in the presence of a freshness and beauty and power that anticipates eternity. I am still and the sea rolls and whirls by with a beauty ever ancient and always new. I sit by the sea in the sun and realize that my happiness is not around the next promontory. It is here and now. I sit quietly as the sea ebbs and flows and know that I sit with God in his world. I know that he sits by my side on my bench by the sea, on that shining golden beach by the blue, blue sea.

It is then that I can hear Jesus saying: "I am not coming, my friend. I am here, and you shall never be alone again."

> Jesus, give me the time to sit still. Stop my rushing about so that I can find you right here and now in my life. I need not wait for your coming. I need only stop my going, my crazy attempt to escape my precious time of waiting with you for the new manifestation of your will.

"All Gone! . . . Oh, There He Is!"

There are some days when I am terribly troubled that God seems to be hiding a secret from me. But Paul in Eph 3:3 assures me that this is the case. God has a secret and part of the secret is that his love for Israel extends to me. The chosen race is the human race. I am chosen as much as anybody else. When I am waiting for him these thoughts are helpful. But they don't answer the question why God himself should sometimes be a secret for me. If he has chosen me, why does he hide himself from me? Could it be that he is playing a game with me? He may just be playing the children's game, "All gone! . . . Oh, there he is!"

I saw a baby play it once long ago. He sat in the middle of a warm living room clutching a favored blanket. When he was sure he had everyone's attention he would cry "All gone!" and hide himself under the blanket's soft darkness. After a few seconds he would throw off the blanket with a cry of glee and we who loved him were expected to shout, "Oh, there he is!" And in that bright warm room we would rejoice together in the discovery of love.

It was a game played out often in the story of Jesus-God. The Chosen People cried after the Messiah, "All gone!" and the pagan Magi laughed, "Oh, there he is!" The first disciples searched for a Master: "All gone!" but the Baptist pointed and said, "Oh, there he is!" Peter and John wept over the empty tomb: "All gone!" but Mary found Jesus in the Easter garden: "Oh, there he is!"

It is a game played in every life. For most of us there are times when Jesus seems so real that we cry with joy, "Oh, there he is!" We touch the fire of God on some days. There is no one method of discovery. For some it will come in the embrace of a loved one. For others it will happen in a precious second of solitude. But however it comes, the secret of God is suddenly revealed, and with John we become conquerors of the world (1 John 5:5). We are convinced that we are loved, that God exists, that Jesus is the Son of God, that God gives us eternal life, that this life is in his Son, that whoever possesses the Son possesses life.

But there are also those times of emptiness, of waiting alone, when every fiber in our being cries out, "All gone!" God seems to be hiding. Beauty is dulled. Love seems far away. We seem to hurt all over and we close in upon ourselves to flee the pain. And we end up waiting for "God-knows-what" in a boring, unlovely world of private agony. We cry, "All gone!" and collapse in upon ourselves. Our only goal is to get through the next day.

Simone Weil writes that these times of waiting, of trying to love in emptiness, are moments of great grace (*Waiting for God,* Harper Colophon Books, 1973, p. 210). It is just at such moments of waiting that we prove our love for the hidden Jesus. There are no rewards. There are no good feelings. There can be only pure love. It is like the love of a spouse for a beloved who has fallen into a coma. There are no sweet words, no gentle touches. There is only the beloved hiding in an immobile body and the love of the one who tends the hiding place.

When Jesus-God is hidden it is a great grace to wait patiently for the day when we can cry in joy, "Oh, there he is!"

> Jesus, give me the strength of the Magi, who continued to search for you during your days of hiding. Give me the wisdom that allowed them to see you in a most unlikely place.

Birth, Love, Death

The days of Christmas time are confusing. But that is good for us. We learn even as children that waiting can lead to a happy absurdity. We learn that we can be filled with joy in the midst of events which don't seem to make much sense.

And so it is that it is good for me to experience Christmas as a time when strange things happen. Things that should not go together suddenly seem to come together. Being born, being in love, dying: all seem to be intertwined. Jesus, born to die from love, seems to say on Christmas that birth and love and death are very much the same.

In life and death and love there is no passage of time. At moments of being born, of falling in love, of dying, Scripture's words about God become true for me: "In his eyes one day is as a thousand years and a thousand years are as a day" (2 Pet 3:8). Time depends on an awareness of past and present and future. For the infant and lover and dying, the only important moment is right now.

In life and in death and in love I am powerless. I had no say whether or not I was to be conceived. God knows, there is no good reason for falling in love. And I have little control over how I shall die. Even doctors and priests must die. And people not particularly lovable are loved. And new fools like me are born every day.

In life and in death and in love I take a leap into darkness. I leap into a new form of life for which I have no precedent. And that is the fearsome part. I am born but once; I will die but once; and each falling in love is radically different.

The Christmas coming of Jesus helps me. The conviction that my Christmas God was born to me out of love for me in order to save me by his death helps to ease my fears. It gives me hope that in my love and in my death I shall be as I was in birth: cradled in the arms of my beloved. Christmas helps me believe that in my loving and dying I will be like a newborn child. It will be as though I were slowly wakening, rubbing sleepy eyes, gradually becoming aware of a grand new world. It is a world discovered at birth in the arms of my mother. It is a world discovered through love in the arms of someone who cares. It is a world revealed in death as I awake in the arms of God. The worlds discovered through birth and love and death will be worlds well worth waiting for.

As I wait now for the coming of Jesus in love and in death I can reflect happily on the wonder of the world he revealed to me in birth. As I wait I can relax in the arms of my beloved God and simply wonder at being alive in such an amazing world where God was born and died because he was so much in love with me. I may only half understand that amazing fact. I may be confused as to what his birth and love and death mean for me. But as I wait for further revelation I will be happy.

> Jesus, let me accept without reservation the life you have given to me; let me embrace without reticence the love you send to me; let me await without fear the death you have prepared for me.

Fantastic Days of Christ's Coming

I remember that Christmas Day was always a fantastic time when I was young. It was a time to be celebrated, and celebration came easily in those innocent days. Somehow now that I am older celebrating fantastic times seems harder. Perhaps it is because fantasy and pleasant dreams depend upon my graceful acceptance of the future and sometimes that becomes more difficult as I grow in age and fears. To celebrate the fullness of *now* I must have faith in *things-yet-to-be*. Without such faith and trust in the future my present party-going tends to be an escape, not a celebration. If I truly celebrate I may forget to drink. If I fear the future I may drink to forget.

I must be comfortable with mystery to be happy about the future. The future for me is always mystery. When I was a child I seemed to accept mystery with more joy. I knew that I did not understand everything but I felt safe in the love of those around me. I was happy because no one seemed to expect me to know everything. I did not need to supply many answers. When I was little I seemed to have the precious right to be dumb. When I grew up things changed. People seemed to expect that I would be in control of things and sometimes their expectations led me to the madness of believing that I was in control of things. Inevitably the day came when I realized that it was madness, that in fact I was in control of very little. I was terrified to discover that I did not have much control even over myself. I was terrified because in my adult pride I lost the ability to have the childhood trust that someone else was in control.

I could not celebrate mystery because I was afraid. Being fearful I could not join the Christians in the wondrous fantasy they play out in their homes, decorating a winter house with fresh greens, wrapping odd gifts in exuberant colors, and pretending that love is the only reality. When I was little this Christmas pageant seemed an appropriate way to celebrate the fantastic coming of Jesus. Later on it was not always easy to join in. There were understandable reasons. How can you imagine wonderful things when you find the present unbearable? How can you avoid terrible nightmares when you must dream in the midst of chaos? How can you dance when you are afraid to walk?

It is sad to be unable to appreciate the fantastic days of Jesus' coming. For those days speak of a fantastic God who became man and now lives with me. They promise that this poor human clod who is me is destined to share forever in God's life. The fantastic days of Christ's coming remind the innocent of the wonders of this world with its millions of living trees to see and touch and smell and climb and swing from and rest under, with its millions of rabbits and bears and walrus and camels and elephants to wonder at, with lots of water to splash and drink and skate on, with lots of air to breathe and huff and puff and whistle.

If I grow with my childhood innocence there is no reason why in my later years I cannot celebrate each new coming of Christ as though it were my first. Jesus tells me every night what loving parents tell their children on Christmas Eve: "You shall sleep and there shall be none to make you afraid" (Lev 26:6). On every morning that Jesus comes to me I can hear the fantastic cry of God: "Come then, my love; my lovely one, come. For see, winter is past, the rains are over and gone. The flowers appear on the earth. The season of glad songs has come" (Cant 2:10-12).

> Jesus, don't let me get so big and so proud that I can't rejoice in the mystery of your birth. I would hate to miss my Christmas because of business supposedly more pressing. Let me be ready to dance and sing when you knock on my door.

Reflections While Waiting for "My Time" to Come

It is easy to write about time on a good "today." To love this today I must be at peace. And so it is with me on this particular day. I am conscious and this is not a burden to me. My body is enjoying the cold snow falling outside this warm room, purring softly over memories of fine meals, lulled by the faraway sounds of the tap-tap typing talk of a busy office. I love today because I am warm and full and not alone.

It is difficult to love today when today is but another day for being cold and hungry. It is difficult to love today when today is but another day for being alone again. The *again* part makes it especially hard. I can accept bad times now if I have some hope that the future will be better. But such hope is unlikely when I am overcome with the memory of unremitting bad times. Apart from a miracle of faith it is impossible to convince a perpetual loser that any victory is possible. Hope is based either on some good memories or on an overpowering faith in someone who can convince us that no matter what has happened or is happening now the future is still open. But even this faith in a person demands some precedent. Before we can believe in a caring person we must believe that it is possible for someone to care. We must have experienced some good to believe in good. Unending affliction destroys hope.

On days of waiting, if you were to ask me what "my time" is, I would not know. I would not want to admit that my time is in fact right now, that my days of waiting are as much my time as are my days of possession. We don't want to live right now if *now* is cold and hungry and lonely. We don't want to live right now if *now* finds us exhausted by remorse or deadened by past pain or crushed by exploded dreams. We don't want to live right now if *now* is pedestrian and unexciting and far less dramatic than our fantasy about the future. It is hard to accept my time as now when I can't get over my past and can't wait for my future.

Wisdom is nothing more than accepting now as my time with all its defects. The wise person is one who can stand to be young, who is willing to be middle-aged, who accepts being old. But it is hard. The environment is frequently against us. We are tempted to primp and paint and punch ourselves out of old age. Children are admonished, "Grow up!" almost as soon as they can understand the words. We in our middle years spend much of our precious time affecting patriarchal wisdom while jogging ourselves into shape, driven by the dream of having the mind of Socrates encased in the body of an Adonis or Venus.

The pity of it all is that we cannot be true to ourselves, much less to anyone else, if we cannot even tell our own time. If this is for me a time of waiting, then wait I must. In trying to snatch some other time I lose myself. I leave my proper place and become lost to those who love me. I become lost to myself. And how can I hope to find the Lord when I cannot even find myself? The wisdom of Eccl 3:1-9 should be written in our hearts, to be read and reread during days of waiting:

> For everything there is a season, and a time for every matter under heaven:
> a time to be born, and a time to die;
> a time to plant, and a time to pluck up what is planted;
> a time to kill, and a time to heal;
> a time to break down, and a time to build up;
> a time to weep, and a time to laugh;
> a time to mourn, and a time to dance;
> a time to cast away stones, and a time to gather stones together;
> a time to embrace, and a time to refrain from embracing;
> a time to seek, and a time to lose;
> a time to keep, and a time to cast away;
> a time to rend, and a time to sew;
> a time to keep silence, and a time to speak;
> a time to love, and a time to hate;
> a time for war, and a time for peace.

There is a time to be young, a time to be middle-aged, a time to be old. There is a time to possess and a time to wait. And all times are grace-filled. Jesus can find me at *any* time as long as it is truly *my* time. There is a time for waiting just as there is a time for everything else. And every time is the time of Christ.

> Jesus, help me to accept this day with all its joys and sorrows. It is my day. I will try to wait for you here and not wander off. I know that you will come in your own good time to reveal yourself to me anew. Give me the patience to wait here at home in this precious time you have given to me alone.

Playing While We Wait

We never cease to be children. We never cease to need some time to play and someone to play with. We need time to be frivolous, a time when there are no world-shaking goals to be accomplished and no complicated evaluations to describe our success or failure. A time of play has no time for losers or winners. It is simply an open time for doing anything and nothing.

When I was a child I played most of the time and through that play I learned fantasy and reality. Later on I was told that play could be childish and should be viewed with suspicion. Play became acceptable if it was disguised as serious work with rules and teams and practices and goals and uniforms to prove that I *belonged*. Running for joy could be indulged in only if it was described as jogging for health. Vacations became chores. Temptations to play became "morose delectations" bearing burdens of guilt if entertained. Sometimes it seems now that there isn't *any* time for play, much less a *good* time.

But in fact any time is a good time for play, even our days of waiting. The Christian liturgy goes so far as to invite us to play right in the middle of Advent, when we wait for the birth of Jesus, and in the middle of Lent, when we wait for his death and resurrection. The play of anticipation can be the best kind. Children play very nicely waiting for good things to come. The eve of great feasts is a fine time for peaceful play with friends, sharing delicious dreams of the wonders soon to appear. Long ago when I sometimes found hidden presents on the days before Christmas, the thinking about them and the looking at the gaily decorated packages was almost as much fun as opening them up. It was sometimes more fun. My dreams of anticipation were always about things I truly wanted. The reality of the gifts (especially when they turned out to be "practical" items) was not as satisfying.

Anticipating a good to come can even help us bear a temporary sorrow. It was possible to play on Thanksgiving, waiting in hunger. And even the passage through death can be traversed merrily if we are certain of resurrection soon to come. Nature wept on Good Friday with the pangs of birth that brought to humanity the final proof of eternal life. The tears were tears of joyous pain.

Days of anticipation, then, can be and should be days of play. It will be a quiet time because there is not yet present the ecstasy of dreams fulfilled. But it will be true play because it is rooted in a confident hope of miraculous things yet to come.

Any time of waiting is a good time for play if we have hope and someone to wait with, someone who can join our play. Indeed, it is much easier to play when we have someone to play with, someone to be foolish with, someone to be completely undignified with. We need someone with whom we can giggle as we match imaginings, letting free spirits mix and separate as they dance through silly conversations. As we wait we need someone to match our cries of glee as though we still were little children gloriously rolling over and over down a daisy-goldened springtime hill. Of course we always could use someone to hold us protectively when things are bad; but we also need someone to play with when things are looking up. It seems to be God's will. In Scripture we are told that after the serious business of the day we should "hurry home to play and do what [we] have a mind to" (Sir 32:16).

The delightful message hidden in Scripture is that Jesus not only saved us; he wants us to play with him, to be with him before the throne of the Father as he "delights him day after day, ever at play in his presence, at play everywhere in his world, delighting to be with the sons of men" (Prov 8:30-31). Perhaps that is why Jesus commands us to be like little children. That is the meaning of his command to love each other as he has loved us, as the Father has loved him (John 15:9).

Jesus has given us a method of waiting. He will surely come. This he promises. And while we wait for that great day we have his permission to play. As we wait we must love each other as he has loved us, playfully. As we wait for him we have his permission to be foolish together, dancing lightly in a spring meadow, diving together through a summer's surging surf, rolling hand in hand through autumn leaves, helping each other build smiling snow giants on the lawns of winter.

As I wait for Jesus I am commanded to love and play, and for good reason. Even now I am in God's house, the universe built by his own hand. And Jesus hides upstairs, chuckling in glee as he waits to join humanity's joyous game.

> Jesus, as I wait for you, give me the assurance that
> you will come soon. Give me a friend so that I need
> not wait alone. Help us play quietly through our days
> of waiting until you come and we all rejoice together.

The Need for a Hug

Each time Jesus comes to me it is like a new birth, both for him and for me. Like a newborn I need to be hugged.

All of us are conceived in peaceful silence and remain at peace in our early months. We are embraced by our mother's womb. The quiet is broken only by her surging heart supporting mother and child through months of fragile growth. I, like others, was born at peace. But it quickly ended. I was snatched from my mother's hug and thrust into a glaring antiseptic room where roamed a white-masked band of giants. A stranger cried, "He weeps! He must be alive!" I wept indeed, but not from physical distress. My tears flowed from my first experience of being alone. I was no longer hugged.

Most of us get a share of hugging as we grow up, but not as much as we could use. The experts command, "Don't spoil the child! Don't pick him up just because he cries." And we think to ourselves, "Why not? Isn't weeping a good reason for a comforting hug?" As time goes on those around us try to convince us that hugging is a waste of precious time. One can't philosophize during a truly fine hug. A good hug takes our breath away and forces us to keep our mouth shut. And society can't stand that. Sophistication demands that we talk more and hug less. If we hug at all we must be sure to do it at appropriate times in appropriate places. We hug in a most reserved and rational way. And we are increasingly sad, because we dimly understand that there are some events in life that can be borne only in the silent embrace of a loved one.

How, for example, can we convince someone of our love? How can we bear the sorrow of a loved one's death? Through words? But that is madness! There are some things that can be said only by embracing in silence, standing with someone who cares and simply holding each other in ecstasy or despair, trying to be with each other at a moment which is inexpressible. We pray together that the joy will never go or that the sorrow will quickly pass. Our embrace does not guarantee that our prayers will come true. But it does get us through. We get by with a hug and a prayer.

And thus it is that I am indeed blessed as I wait for Jesus' revelation in my life if I can experience some sort of loving hug. In that experience of love I can wait for the new coming of faith. In that experience of love I can hope. Jesus is where love is. As I wait blindly I am like a newborn child who cannot yet see but is already embraced. As I wait for Jesus I am already embraced by that God who soon shall be revealed to me.

> Jesus, on those confusing days when I must wait for your guidance, get someone to hug me. Embrace me through them, so that as I wait I will not be frightened.

The Search for Love and Faith

The turtle is a fine animal to help me make sense of my days of discovery. I like camels also but for other reasons that I will not go into here. But a turtle is a fine image for the days when I was a little "tad" looking for something to believe in and someone to love. The turtle spends a lot of time when on land staying in one place. He looks around with unsmiling face for something to happen. Or simply withdraws into himself and waits in fear. As long as he peers and fears he makes little movement. It is not until he gets to the sea that he begins to cavort and dance, not looking for anything especially new, just rejoicing in what he has. Turtles are born on land and apparently few ever make the sea. They spend so much time hiding within themselves or looking around for certain directions that they never get anyplace.

And so it is with us when we are young (and sometimes when we are old) and looking for something to believe in and something to love. We take the search so seriously that we can't recognize the share of faith and love that is ours. We worry so much about what we have that it quickly goes sour. We find it hard to be natural in our faith or in our love. We find it hard to be childlike.

The life of the child is in many ways a fine life. When a little girl loves, she loves. When she is frightened, she cries. When she is angry, she yells. She moves from emotion to emotion without guilt, without reservation. There is no embarrassment in what she has or has not. She marches jay-bird naked through the living room to visit with friends, thinking nothing of it. We on our part cry out with frightened laughter, "Go upstairs and put your clothes on!" afraid that if such naturalness caught on it might mark the end of civilization.

And thus it is that we spend more time worrying about love than being in love. We worry about what can go wrong or what other people will say rather than simply saying to our beloved, "We have found love! Let us rejoice in it! Let us gambol a bit through a convenient field!" We think we have faith and immediately question it. "Do I really believe?" we say, and forget that the question is one that does not admit of answer. Faith and love cannot stand too much analysis. Ultimately they are decisions, and energy spent in analysis is lost to the strengthening of our commitment. In waiting for some private transfiguration in which Jesus-God will take me up some private mountain to reveal himself especially to me, I lose the opportunity to walk with the ordinary Jesus who is knocking on my shell trying to get me to stick my head out.

It comes down to this: we all leave spores as we pass through life, turtle trails in the sands of history. Perhaps the best thing to do is to get on with my journey with all the love and faith I can muster right now. At least then I may leave a modest trail of love and joy behind me as I continue my search for that perfect love and final faith (which probably don't exist anyway here on the beach).

One sure thing: it does no good at all to pull in my legs, bow my head, and hide in my shell as I wait for some final solution. There is no room for Jesus in such narrow confines. And he probably wouldn't come if he could. (Have you ever smelled a hiding turtle?) And I wouldn't get much love either. There would be nothing showing to kiss.

Come on, Jesus, let's take a run for the sea! As we progress you may help me see more clearly. But in any case I'm better off running than hiding.

When Christmas Comes in Springtime

I remember the spring of my life, when I was in my late teens and early twenties, as a time when I truly felt good. All my parts seemed to be in working order and they meshed without pain. I was running without agony, sleeping easily, and beginning each day with fire. It is true that I may not have had much sense when I was eighteen, but I certainly did feel good.

Days of youth and health are fine days to wait for the coming of Christ. My family had provided me with roots. Now they were giving me wings. My old family loves were still there but they were not suffocating. The loves of my childhood did not hold me back from new adventures. They encouraged me and gave me the confidence to try the unknown. These were days for seeking new life and new places. As yet there was no place that was truly mine but this was because every place was equally attractive and equally possible. Nor was there any one special person to whom I had vowed my future. Old loves understood that I needed to move on and I was committed to no one with whom I would share my life. I cared for everyone. I truly believed that the future would be filled with interesting events and lovely people. I was ready to fly.

Such days of healthy, confident youth are perhaps the closest we come to a heaven on earth. As I understand it, in heaven this old body will truly "feel good." I will look forward with joy to an infinite space and an infinite time in which to discover the good things the Lord has prepared for me. It will be even better than being eighteen because I will have the fullness of "feeling good" without the anxiety of youth. I won't have a fear of growing old. I will not have the desperate desire to "make my mark." I will know what I am. I will know that I will never change. And I will be satisfied in knowing that I am secure in the love of Jesus-God. I will feel "really good." .

The coming of Jesus had a very special meaning in the springtime of my life. Christmas in those days marked the coming of a great good friend who would share my journey to unknown places among unknown people. He would be interested in my tasks. He would help me as much as he could but even more he would always be willing to sit with me at the end of a long day to talk about how things were going. It seemed as though that God whom I had known in my childhood as a protector was coming now as a friend. The Christmas message of my youth was the same as always: "He comes!" but it had a different meaning. That God-child whom I had previously adored was coming now as a man to share my adult dreams. When Christmas came in the springtime of my life it was easy to understand the joyful cry of Zephaniah:

> Sing aloud, O daughter of Zion;
>   shout, O Israel!
> Rejoice and exult with all your heart, . . .
> The Lord your God is in your midst, . . .
> he will rejoice over you with gladness,
> he will renew you in his love;
> he will exult over you with loud singing
>   as on a day of festival (3:14; 17-18).

In the springtime when Jesus came, both he and I felt "really good."

Jesus, give me the joy of running with you in my youth, talking with you in later years, and resting with you in death. Christmas can come at any season.

2   Ordinary Days

Green is the color of my ordinary days. These are those middle years when I am not particularly young or particularly old. It is as though I am floating on a noon sea. My sun is still, neither rising nor setting. These are emerald days when I celebrate my present. I do not look back with nostalgia because the "good old days" are here. I do not view my past with any burden of guilt because past mistakes can still be undone or forgiven. I do not particularly long for a better future. Many of my hopes have already been fulfilled and I have a stable base on which to prepare for any changes that may come. My life is neither aggravating nor boring. If love has come, it still seems fresh and new. If it has not yet arrived, there still is time.

The green of these ordinary days provides a soft background on which to write my story. The times are placid. I float through my days as on a calm sea. I am aware of but not disturbed by the gentle lapping of passing events and people. My days are marked by constancy. Of course there are some storms. They are impressive for an instant but they die swiftly, leaving only gentle swells to mark their passage. But most times the days are so still that it seems as though I am becalmed in blue-green ice. My only temptation is to sleep my way to oblivion.

I am not alone. Special friends float with me for a time and we hold hands. The moving currents remind me that such intimacy will not be forever. I realize that at any moment they or I could sink through the green swells to be consumed by the depths of God. I believe in contingency but it seems to be a long way off. During these gentle green ordinary days it is easy to think that I and my friends will be together forever.

Green is a color filled with hope, and a quiet hope supports my heart as I go through these days. I am very lucky. I feel surrounded by love. I suspect that Jesus-God is somewhere near. Certainly my ordinary days are not all sweetness and light but they are mostly good. And even on bad days it is still possible to laugh a little. As I float on the cool green sea of my ordinary days I feel very, very lucky.

A Day by the Sea

It was a sunny day at a summer beach. It seemed specially created for the young people who played in the surf or rested in warm isolation on the yellow sand, skin gradually dying to a satisfactory brown. The day was filled with youth and brightness and fine things to see. There was, however, something out of place.

She sat on a bench drinking iced tea given by the friend who sat by her side. She seemed a stranger to the scene around her. In the midst of all that youth she was old. In the midst of all that whiteness she was black. In the midst of that seashore feast of fine sights she was blind.

For a moment I felt terribly sad but then it struck me that she seemed at peace. She seemed to be enjoying the cool of the drink, the warmth of the sun, the smell of the sea, the laughter of the children passing by. She needed only to reach out her arm to touch someone who cared that she was alive. In a way she was happier than some with sight who could see that they were alone.

Seeing her there sipping her tea, smiling towards the sound of her attentive friend, helped me appreciate the colors of my day. I remembered that I too had those who cared about me. Suddenly I was awash in joy.

If Jesus had walked by, perhaps he would have cured her. It is more likely that he simply would have sat down and enjoyed her company for a while, sipping tea and talking with her and her dear friend. Jesus knows that it is better to be blind and loved than to have sight and hang on a cross alone. That is the reason he sometimes leaves us sightless but will never leave us alone.

Jesus, be with me in my waking and in my sleeping, in my light and in my darkness. Help me rejoice in the

25

gifts you have given me. Help me know that you are there in my good times and in my bad times.

My Body and Me

My body is a mixed blessing. Some days I hate it. Some days I love it. It can be aggravating. It stays up too late, won't go to sleep, but refuses to get up in the morning. Mostly it is weak, demanding extreme efforts to prevent it from falling apart. It is often ugly. It is difficult to realize sometimes as I peer glumly into my morning mirror that under that flabby flaccid flesh beats a heart of gold and shines a mind sharp as a shining sword. It sometimes humiliates me. When I am winning the race of life it tires. When I am pretending to be cool and calm it perspires. And when I am finally ready to reach out and grab the golden ring of success, it expires. On some days I understand those body-bothered humans throughout history who have cried: "I am not my body! I am stuck with it but it is not me. Because I am strong and it is weak; I am pretty and it is ugly; I am exalted and it is lowly. 'Cogito, ergo sum!' 'I think, therefore I am!' 'Corpus mea, pondus meum!' 'My body is my burden!'"

On other days I feel quite comfortable with the ratty old thing. When it feels good, I feel good. And it teaches me some good truths. I first learned what it means to have a hunger satisfied at my mother's breast. The amazing fact that my physical hunger could be satisfied dried my baby tears. It gave me hope. If that belly-pain could be relieved, so too could the deeper hunger of my spirit. My body helps me understand what total giving in human love is like. Human love is not simply a union of flesh but neither is it only a mating of minds. The ecstasy of union can help a couple understand why their marriage is "two becoming one."

Indeed, even when it feels poorly I have an attachment for the mangy, coughing, bilious thing that sometimes is my body. I put it to bed lovingly when it is ill, convinced beyond all doubt that Plato was wrong and that indeed my body is a part of me. I am not soul. I am embodied soul. I have no inkling of what life without body might be like. And that is the cause of my difficulties in being convinced about immortality. For how can I believe that this mangy body will last forever? Only through the testimony of Jesus-God.

And to this he has testified. My body is not a passing fancy. It will be with me forever and not as a burden to be borne. Because it is in and through my body that I shall be saved. Jesus proclaims, "I am God!" "You are saved!" "You shall rise again!" His message is a cause for singing for me and my body.

> Jesus, bless my body in its splendor and in its infirmity. Help me overcome its sometimes madness when satisfaction is its burning passion. Help me live with its illness in patience and hope. You saved me through the crucifixion of your body. Let mine too be an instrument of salvation.

Trying to Get Going

I am inert. I have energy to do nothing. Trying to move about the room I trip over myself. My parts will not wake up. I feel like a rational amoeba, just a glob and conscious of the fact. Paul must have had a morning like this when he wrote: "While we live in this earthly tent we groan with a feeling of oppression. It is not that we want to get rid of our earthly body, but that we want to have the heavenly one put on over us so that what is mortal will be swallowed up by life" (2 Cor 5:4). He probably wrote that on a morning when he got up and found that his foot would not work, that his tent creaked.

On such mornings when my tent creaks I think to myself, "My God, if now that I am healthy I cannot get moving, how in the world shall I bear illness?" And so I rub oil on my cracking surface, flap out the tent walls, warm it up, and exercise it so that I can be in contact with the rest of the world.

Of course I don't need a good tent to be in contact with God. That happens inside. Indeed maybe death will be like this: I will become more and more involved with God inside the tent. I withdraw more and more into him until finally there is nothing left inside my old tent walls. As evening approaches I will forget to light the usual warming candle inside and the tent will finally collapse, its flatness testifying that indeed I am gone off and running somewhere else with Jesus.

But right now I don't feel as though I am dying as I sit here on my stool looking vacantly at the slowly lightening dawn of another day of work. I just can't seem to move my foot. Here I am supposed to go out and conquer the world but just now I can't muster the energy to tie my shoe! And so I sit here a bit longer wishing with Paul not necessarily to get rid of this old tent but at least to pep it up with some sort of "lube" job and perhaps a resurfacing. In any case the question remains: "How can I save the world today if I can't even get my foot to move?"

Jesus, did you ever have days when you could not get moving? I suspect that you did since your human tent was not that much different from mine. I hope you will understand me on my days of inertia, days when the greatest victory is not falling down as I lurch through my tasks. On such days I don't think I care about you less. I just can't get my foot to move.

Mother's Love: God's Love

Now that I am big I can say some sensible things about my mother. When I was little I was too busy hiding behind her leg to do much writing. Of course I loved my father too and he was my protector from all my big enemies, like the Communists and the Martians. But my mother took care of the dog next door, who loved to feed on me, and the bully up the street, who loved to beat on me, and the terrible monsters who would wake up with me in the dead of night. If my mother had been into slacks she would have needed a pair with three legs, one for each of her own and one for her youngest who spent much of his youth grafted to her.

Now I understand that although both my mother and father are responsible for the wonder that is me, my mother had a special place. She not only generated me, she bore me, and then put up with me for the rest of her life. She risked her life to give me a chance to see light. For nine months she supported the two of us on a somewhat tenuous thread. There was a chance, especially at the end, that the thread would break and both of us would perish. As it was, when I was finally delivered to the uncaring world, I took much of her with me. She could easily have died giving me life.

My mother's heart was the first sound I heard. As a child I trembled to think that someday that great heart would stop. Where would I be then? I spent my early years nestling to her breast or perched on her shoulder or balanced on her hip or clinging to her leg, finding always the softness that I needed to bear the hardnesses of life. I knew that I could always come back to that softness after the bruising combats of my small life's playgrounds.

And so it is for most of us growing up. When we get big we try to reject all that romantic nonsense. We men especially cry that we are rough and tough and don't need softness any more. We play football and yell a lot. We speak knowingly of the dog-eat-dog world and strut and pose and generally make jackasses of ourselves. Because with all our noise we desperately search for someone who will care about us half as much as did our mothers, someone who will wipe away our tears when we return bruised and hurt from those adult playgrounds we call our careers. The simple fact is that no matter how big we are or how old we are we never cease to be children. We always need the affection and soft concern given us first by our mothers. We spend a lifetime seeking it.

The wondrous message of Scripture is that God wants to be that perfect lover for us, embracing us with all our human loves forever. Thus Isaiah hears God say:

> Can a mother forget her infant,
> be without tenderness for the child of her womb?
> Even should she forget,
> I will never forget you (49:15).

God tells Zechariah:

> Whoever touches you touches the apple of my eye (2:12).

In the book of Revelation a loud voice from God's throne speaks of the Lord's dwelling among us at the end of time:

> He shall dwell with them and they shall be his people and he shall be their God who is always with them. He shall wipe every tear from their eyes (21:3-4).

No wonder, then, that the psalmist happily affirms:

> Though my father and mother forsake me,
> yet will the Lord receive me (27:10).

If we are lucky the taste of mother-love creates a thirst to seek love wherever we go. Again if we are lucky (and I bless my God that I have been so), we find human loves to carry us through most of our days. We are drawn irresistibly from the arms of our mothers through the embraces of the loves that support us in later life until finally in ecstasy we leap into the arms of God. It sounds strange at first that God is drawing us to himself through all our true human loves but it was prophesied long ago by Hosea:

> I will draw them to me with the cords of Adam,
> with the bands of love (11:4).

I can wait for God with confidence knowing that just as I began life in the warm embrace of the finite womb of my mother, just as I have lived my life in the supporting love of good friends, so shall I live my eternity in the maternal embrace of God.

> Jesus, thank my mother for her gift of love to me.
> Through it I came to recognize my need for love and
> the assurance that someone could love me. This need
> drove me to search for you. This assurance of human
> love made it seem possible that I could even be loved
> by God.

Days of Sadness: Days of Play

One Friday afternoon I watched a young boy die. It was in a bright white room, quiet except for muffled hospital sounds and the city far below grumbling over the task of going home.

On the next morning I watched a baby play on an ocean beach colored all brilliant yellow and blue and pink. The morning sounds were those of a world at peace with itself and of a child laughing at gulls calling high above.

My Saturday's child sang as she went about her little tasks, piling tiny white pebbles in the trapped ocean's emerald pools, chasing sandpipers at the water's edge. She laughed because the day was fine and she was surrounded by love. She knew that she would be forever safe in the arms of those who loved her. I ran with her on that morning beach and Jesus danced to see our joy.

My Friday's child was also loved. He was not alone. Family and friends were there to be with him through his earthly life's last great event. We were sad because of imminent parting. Jesus came with his sacrament. And he wept with the rest of us because a child was about to die.

Indeed, Jesus-God cares very much what happens to his children. But sometimes it is hard to understand. Oh, we have no problem with Jesus dancing with a little girl on a golden ocean beach. But how are we to fathom him when he stands helpless in a bright white room listening to the strained gasping of his child, hearing the weeping of the family as their boy slips off to sleep, waking no more in this life? Doesn't Jesus-God care?

Scripture tells us that he cares for all of his children. After all, he was a child himself and knows the special joy of playing like a child. Probably he didn't have much time to do things like play "catch." His foster father, the good man Joseph, died early and Jesus had to support his mother. He didn't have much time to play ball or go to the beach, but we know he would have liked to. He was a child.

Later on, when he grew up, he told his friends that they should try to become children again before they died. Only children enter heaven because only children have the simple unworried love that is the key. Perhaps if I were more childlike I could more easily see the connection between the death of Friday's child and the dance of Saturday's child.

Now that the sorrow has dulled I can see that the two events are not unrelated. Just as that Saturday's baby, so recently removed from the quiet darkness of a womb's love-embrace, rejoiced in the colors and sounds and smells of the new bright world, so too did Friday's child leave the loves of this sometimes gray old world to join Jesus in the sights and sounds and smells of a truly new fine bright world.

Why does a child die? Why do any of us die? Perhaps because Jesus needs someone to dance with.

Jesus, I know you love children. I know you love
all my little friends. But be patient! Don't take them

off dancing too soon, leaving me behind. Give me more time to play with them here on this world's beaches before we go our separate ways. Better still, why don't you come and play with us here for a time? Afterwards we can go to your house together.

Quiet Days of Listening

There are some days when I need to sit back and listen to life, to be with others quietly hearing them. Such days are those when I can't sort myself out too well, when I have few answers and am not too sure of the questions. Certainly it does no good at such times to go out to those I love with my confusions. It would serve no purpose except to mess up their lives. Better by far to be quiet while Jesus and I try to get my house in order.

In the meantime I can still listen to others and enjoy them. I can listen as I wait for the dust to settle here inside me. As I rest within myself I wait for the whisper of God, for he is here inside me.

My state is not one of apathy nor even of passivity. I still listen, visiting with others in the places where they may be. I am alert, listening for the sound of God, encouraged by the prayer of Augustine:

> Late have I loved you, O Beauty so ancient and so new, late have I loved you. And behold you were inside me all the time, while I was searching outside. I threw myself into your creation looking for you and did not find you. Indeed these things outside me held me back from finding you. You called out and cried and burst in upon my deafness (*Confessions,* bk. 10, ch. 27).

It would be nice to find a perfect place for listening, perhaps a placid sea. But at least I can strive for an internal quiet so that I may hear the voice of others and perhaps the voice of God.

Jesus, help me to be quiet today. It is your turn to talk now.

Days of Passion

I share the very human tendency to "play it cool." Perhaps that's why I ended up in philosophy rather than chemistry (where I began). Errors in my philosophy will not be destructive till long after I am gone. My abortive chemistry career has already caused the death of several labs. On most days I try to keep loose, not getting involved so deeply in any venture as to close off avenues of escape. I think I am not alone in such caution. Humans in their loves are tempted to play the field and stay ready to separate at the first taste of sourness. Humans in their lives are constantly looking over fences and are prepared to change careers (if they can) at the first touch of boredom. We humans like to skim lightly over the surface of our calling. We are seldom possessed by it. We frequently think of how it would have been in the supposedly greener grass of the other person's pasture. We are tempted to be safe in all that we do. All passion is eliminated from our lives and later on we die, with no one noticing the difference.

If we are lucky we avoid becoming part of the living dead by experiencing some days of passion, days on which we are touched by a consuming fire. Usually it is in the form of a fiery love for some cause or some human or some god. Whatever its object it is painful to body and soul. In agony and delight we cry out as Jeremiah cried when touched by God's love:

> You duped me, O Lord, and I let myself be duped:
>> you were too strong for me, and you triumphed . . .
> I say to myself, I will not mention him,
>> I will speak in his name no more.
> But then it becomes like fire burning in my heart,
>> imprisoned in my bones;
> I grow weary holding it in,
>> I cannot endure it (20:7, 9).

"I CANNOT ENDURE IT!" is the cry of a person on the day of passion.

Paul says that to be alive as Christians we must "offer our living bodies as a holy sacrifice" (Rom 12:1). To come close to divine love we must be prepared to chance being consumed, to chance being reduced to exhausted ashes. We touch God only on days of passion. And we cannot have such days if we deaden our lives by always trying to be safe.

Peter was trying to "play it cool" when he advised Christ not to go out on a limb by going up to Jerusalem (Matt 16:21). Christ's response was swift and cutting and almost frenzied. His words to Peter are meant for me too:

> Get out of my sight, you devil! You are trying to make me fail! You are not inspired by the fire of God but by the fear of man. What in God's name are you saving yourself for? If you spend all your time trying to protect your life, if you never go out on a limb for love of a man or a woman or a cause or a god, what have you to protect? You are dead, my friend! You are already dead!
>
> So come one, come all! Join me in my mad dance of love celebrating the fact that humanity is important, that God is important, that there are some things in life worth working for and worth dying for!
>
> What does it matter that you are consumed by your life and love? At least as you leap with passion into eternity you will be able to cry out to those cool plodding souls left behind: "Goodbye, my friends! I must leave you now, because I have discovered what it means to be on fire with life, I have discovered what it means to be on fire with love, and now I must go to be consumed by the passion of God!"

When Christ ended his words he turned with determination and strode up the road that led to Jerusalem and death. And only those able to feel passion followed him.

> Jesus, give me days of passion on which I care enough about someone or something to die for them. Let me exercise my passion on things and people around me so that some day I will recognize the full passion of love for you. Don't let me be foolish in my passions. But some days let me be passionate. It will be good for me.

Valentine's Day

Valentine was a priest who was martyred in the third century. This is the fact, somewhat dull and hardly cause for our romantic fervor on February 14th. An ancient tradition (which may or may not be true) is more to the point. According to this story Valentine, on the night before his death, remembering all his friends, took a stone shaped like a heart and scraped on it the words: "To those who love me, to those I love, take my heart and know that I have loved you till the end." He dropped the heart from his prison window to the street below and went off to his death. It is a fine story but in my younger days I found it somewhat scary. I thought to myself, "Suppose I did something like that and got no response! Suppose I mailed out the message 'To whom it may concern: I love you,' only to have it returned stamped 'Addressee Unknown.'" It would be terrible to have one's heart auctioned off by the Post Office as an unclaimed package. In those days I was afraid to give my heart, lest it be lost forever. I was afraid to love.

Now I realize that it is not all that bad. Jesus has given me permission to love and be loved. Indeed, according to John, Jesus insists on it: "Dear friends! Let us love one another, for love comes from God. Whoever loves is a child of God and knows God. Whoever does not love does not know God, because God is love" (John 4:7-8). But to love is hard sometimes. For one reason or another we sometimes feel incapable of loving. On some days we do not feel lovable at all.

I still remember my first day in school. There I was, a small tyke sitting in the back of the room surrounded by enemies of like size, recently cast off by my mother who left me at the door with a sigh which sounded suspiciously like an expression of relief (as the youngest of seven I discovered that the romance of children had long since dissipated from my parents' attitude). In any case, there I was alone in the back of the class looking up to the front at a nun who seemed as big as the Empire State Building! I thought to myself, "Oh Lord, what did I get into?" There I was, a stupid ugly kid thrust into a world of strangers! I felt like Isaiah, unworthy of any kiss. "Woe is me, I am doomed! For I am a man of unclean lips, living among a people of unclean lips" (6:5). Especially felt I thus after one of my compatriots bit my newly vaccinated arm, which quickly became infected.

On that first day of school, facing the towering Sister of St. Joseph, I felt like nothing. It was one of those days when humans feel fit for no good thing because they are too young or too old or too little or too big or too stupid or too smart. It was hard to believe on my first day of first grade that I was lovable in any way at all. Later on, of course, when I discovered that Sister Cornelia *loved* me, she could not get me out of her hair. Whenever she had an errand to run, I joined the other kids (and Isaiah) in the cry, "Here I am, send me!" (Isa 6:9)

Our reluctance in the face of love may be caused by memories of the injuries we have inflicted. We have loved in the past and with passion, but it did not work out. In one way or another we failed our love. When love is offered again we react with surprise, like Paul when he wrote: "Finally Jesus came to me as one born out of normal course. I am the least of the apostles; in fact, because I persecuted the church of God, I do not even deserve the name" (1 Cor 15:1-11). We have acted like persecutors by stealing the love belonging to the Lord or a dear human friend. Now we feel that we can never love them again. We can never go back to our dear Lord or our dear friend because we have crucified them.

I remember feeling that way about a girl on our block. When I was eleven I used to hoot and holler at her with the other boys in my gang, calling her such ugly things as "girl," making fun of her because she was not like us boys. Naturally when I was twelve I fell madly in love with her. But how could I tell her of my love? How could I, her persecutor, now give her my heart? I solved the problem by sending her unsigned love notes written in lemon juice, the nearest thing at hand to invisible ink. Of course she never responded. But at least I had the satisfaction of knowing I had done no further injury to my love, beyond the puzzlement that must still strike her remembering that period when she was besieged by blank pieces of paper addressed with obvious passion to her.

As we grow older and experience our fair share of failure in life we develop new reasons for not loving. Having failed in life and love in the past we are pessimistic about any new ventures, romantic or otherwise. We feel like poor Peter having fished all day without catching anything. At the end of such days how dare we offer our heart to the Lord or to anyone else? Who wants the gift of a loser? Much better by far to go off to our solitary corner, lick our wounds, and not run the risk of failing again.

One of my friends in high school must have felt that way after the prom. We were supposed to go together. Both of us had fine girls but no "wheels." Luckily our ways parted before he came up with his solution. He worked part-time at St. Joseph's home for wayward girls. Since he was a good and faithful soul the authorities were happy to lend him one of the school vehicles for his grand date. In glory he drove his beloved up to the front of the Ben Franklin Hotel, escorting her into the lobby with a flourish. He never saw her again. Only afterwards did he notice that emblazoned on the side of his princess' carriage were the words: ST. JOSEPH'S HOME FOR WAYWARD GIRLS. Certainly it was a failure, but it was not the end of his life. On that very night he discovered his vocation to the religious life.

Our past failures, the injuries we have brought to our beloved, our own supposed ugliness: none of these are good reasons for withdrawing our heart from others. Our love is one of the few things in life that we are in control of. It can be given freely. And it is important. The only reason we were created was to give love to the Lord and to each other. Decrepit as our love may be, there is no one else's like it. It reflects the Lord in its own special way. We are made in our unique way because each of us is destined by God to proclaim his glory in a unique way and to break through the shell of solitude imprisoning those around us whom only we can touch.

We can't claim to be "no-account" because (as the saying goes) God does not make junk. Even the fact that we have previously hurt our love does not stand in the way of giving again. Each day is a new day of possibility. Past injuries may make it difficult for our human dear ones to accept our love right away. But it does not stand in the way of our giving it. And eventually it usually happens that our injured loves are worn down by our persistence and they forgive, if not forget. With the Lord past injuries do not stand in the way at all. He embraces those who are nailing him to the cross. And failures don't bother him either. Peter was not very successful as a fisherman. But he did fairly well as the first head of the Church. Jesus sometimes sees things in us that we cannot see ourselves.

We don't know that much about Valentine except that he died for the Lord. The story about the heart may be false, and indeed probably is. But it is a good story nonetheless. We know that Valentine died in the arms of the Lord. And it was Jesus who in truth sent the very first valentine from Golgotha, saying to the world: "To those I love, take my heart and know that I have loved you till the end." Perhaps that's where Valentine got his idea.

Jesus, help me not to run from love for foolish reasons. I need to love to find you. I need to receive

love to be happy. Help me not to hurt my loved ones.
Help me never to give up on them or you or myself. I
may not be much but I am all you made me. There
must therefore be something fine in me, even on my
most messy days.

A Day for "Holding My Tongue"

There are some days when I feel like shouting, "Is there no one able to hear what I need to say?" These are the days when I must censor my words. These are days for "watching my language" and "holding my tongue." These are days when I must fence with my words lest I injure my friends with truths too harsh for them. These are days when I must fence myself in with my words lest my vulnerable life be exposed to the enemy. Paranoia? Probably, but no less real for all that.

My feelings seem likely to explode. I have a desperate need to show them to someone kind and understanding. The last thing I need as I make my first tentative revelation is the warning: "Watch your language!" Rather, I need someone to say, "Yes, I am listening and I care."

But so often there is no one who can stand my story. There are some who listen for a while and then interrupt before I finish. It is with good intentions mostly. They interrupt because they think they have the final answer to the way I feel (i.e., confused, in love, angry, happy), or they have the best of all possible reasons why I should not feel as I do (i.e., confused, in love, angry, happy). The explanations are seldom very helpful. It is much better to be ignored, to have my friends pass over my problem quickly in order to describe something *really* interesting: namely, *their* problem. When faced with indifference I can at least withdraw my modest trial balloon, close the doors to my heart, and become a listener again. It is easier to be ignored than to be misunderstood. In an environment of indifference it is easier to change the subject without feeling like a fool.

It is a great gift to have a dear friend to whom we can reveal ourselves. It must be a dear friend because somedays only a true lover can stand us as we really are. And no one human being can fulfill the function in every circumstance. Each of us has some element of the truth that is too much to bear, no matter how intensely another may wish to bear it. There are always some secrets to keep even from those we love most deeply. Our love demands that we respect their sensitivity. Some things can be said to cronies that cannot be said to wives. The anonymity of the confessional sometimes supports full revelation. The screen blocks off the surprise or pain that may flicker momentarily in the eyes of the poor human priest who must listen to us in the name of Jesus.

It is sometimes terribly hard to be honest with one we love. This dear friend loves us and hence is more vulnerable to the hurt we inflict. There is, for example, the desire that our love should be perfect. How then can we explain without pain the reality of our feelings? How can we call attention to our doubts, our fears that we are unable to give all that love demands, our confusion about what being in love really means?

St. Paul writes that I am not to sadden the Holy Spirit, that I am never to let evil talk pass my lips, that I am to say only the good things men need to hear, things that will really help them (Eph 4:29-32). If I am to do this, there will necessarily be days of holding my tongue lest its fears and hatreds and hurts escape to do injury to those I love. Of course, as one of my sarcastic friends suggested, I can always "tell it to the Baby Jesus!" But on some days even he seems far away, perhaps taking an afternoon nap as babies are accustomed to do.

> Jesus, when you wake up can I tell you something? Right now there seems to be no one else who is able and willing to listen, understand, and not be hurt. After I tell you my story I promise to be quiet and go back to listening to the important stories of others as they describe how they feel (i.e., confused, in love, angry, happy).

Days of Stumbling Gods

It is truly hard some days to be a parent or some type of authority on whom others lean for support. It is a well-known fact that mothers never get sick, fathers never cry, counselors never get confused, priests never have bad thoughts, and psychiatrists are never crazy. To this, reality replies in stentorian, foghorn tones: *b-r-r-ach!* Even Jesus had a bad night. It was the night before he died. And when God went for someone to help him, when Jesus the comforter went to find comfort, he did not find it. Humanity was otherwise engaged. Our society cannot bear stumbling gods.

All this came back to me the other day when I tried to tell some people how I really felt. My words were like a sermon to the deaf. It was not their fault, of course. It was just that they could not hear what I was saying. Depending so long on my strength, they could not bear my insecurity. "Father knows best," "Deans are good managers," "Philosophers have the inside track on wisdom": all these fallacies stood in the way of this priestly, deanly philosopher revealing the amazing fact that at this particular moment he felt like a little child in the middle of an unknown world. My temptation to reveal this amazing fact soon passed, as does the temptation of mothers to reveal that they are tired to death, and as the temptation of fathers to reveal that they are scared to death soon goes by the board. But the memory lingers. And it convinces me again that we humans are a crazy lot. We cry in rage at fallen angels not because they are fallen but because we suddenly realize that they were never angels at all. And we feel cheated.

That's why we killed Jesus. (I say "we" since there is no reason to suppose that we would have been kinder than the poor folks who lived then.) All of us feel cheated when our gods suffer and stumble. We cry "Blasphemy!" and crucify them in one way or another. Rage and violence are more satisfying than sitting down and listening to a god describe his pain. We can stand watching our gods die because we can transfer our worship to the powers that killed them. But a god who simply is a bit tarnished is too much to bear.

On a day when a god stumbles, when Mom gets sick and Dad gets frightened and the saint sins and the psychiatrist starts acting funny, it would be nice not to curse. It would be nice to have someone catch our fallen gods, just as Mary held Jesus fallen dead from his cross.

> Jesus, give me someone to look up to, another
> human who will be my strong, strong friend. Give me
> someone to love me, another human who will be my
> gentle, gentle friend. Let me carry those who depend

on me with strength as long as I can. Let them understand when I finally fall. And Lord, be with me in my
strength and in my weakness, in my rising but
especially in my falling. Because in my falling there
may not be anyone else but you.

A Fine Time for Dancing

A wedding is a fine time for dancing and, strange as it may seem,
there are never any poor dancers at weddings. It is a grand time for all.
Mothers are permitted to dance with sons, grandfathers with grand-
daughters, big aunts with tiny nieces. Sometimes even old uncles may
be discovered in the lengthening shadows in solitary dance to music
they hum quietly to themselves. There is a mixing of ages as young
foxes slow to a stately trot and old bears risk ultimate hibernation in
frantic disco. Every wedding is a memory of Cana, where rough fisher-
men stomped and clapped and young maidens sang as Jesus danced
with his mother and his friends.

There are those of course who would have you believe that it is un-
Christian to have a good time. They will tell you that to be like Jesus it
is necessary to be sad all the time, or at least very reserved. They paint
the saints with pained facial expressions, which are supposed to repre-
sent sanctity. In truth, for me it is usually a sign of heartburn. These
purveyors of gloom would have us believe that Jesus was always worrying about the cross or planning the great tasks that were ahead. They
take seriously the description of Cana as the place where he did his
first great work. We are supposed to believe he went to the wedding to
do a task. Now I don't wish to discount the wonder of his changing
water into wine (even though some local cafes seem to turn wine into
water every night of the week), but I like to think that he went to the
wedding for the same reasons we go to weddings. He wanted to have a
good time. I must believe that Jesus danced at Cana and thereby
demonstrated by his action that it is not un-Christian to laugh and sing
and dance and be in love. The great message of Cana is that Jesus
knew that a wedding is a fine time for dancing. On that day God had a
great time dancing with his creatures.

It is so easy to forget the joy of life. So often we are rightfully worried about sickness and suffering, about death for ourselves and our loved ones. We are understandably frightened of war and the malice and stupidity of those we cannot trust. We are so upset so often by so many things that it is easy to forget that we were created to be happy. It is easy to forget that we were given legs for dancing as much as for running away in fright. It is easy to forget that Jesus lives and loves and rejoices in us.

Every wedding reminds me of Cana and Cana reminds me that love is just fine and that God loves me certainly and that there are at least a few others who seem to like me too. And that memory takes away some of my worry about not being the right age or the right size or the right anything. Cana tells me that there is no one best way to dance or to love, nor is there one best time for dancing or loving. Love can flourish at the dawn and noon and dusk of life. Perhaps that's why we like to dance at weddings, those great celebrations of human love. We all dance like children when we are in love, and at wedding dances we all are the same age. We are ready and willing to dance with anybody, even Jesus. And who knows, perhaps those old uncles shuffling happily away in the dark corners of the dance floor are not in solitary dance after all. For God knows that weddings are fine times for dancing, and he is always ready to take his turn and rejoice with his creatures.

Jesus, can I dance with you next? Any song they play will be our song. I want to laugh with you for a while.

Days of Foolish Daring

In one of his sermons (I am told) St. Augustine makes reference to the scriptural image of Satan being chained in the desert. He comments on how silly it is to go to see him, remarking: "Only a fool is bitten by a chained dog." Augustine had every right to be rueful about the image. He carried teeth marks all over his hide from the jaws of fierce passions freely embraced. He had bad bruises from troubles he went searching for, knowing full well that nothing good would come from it.

And so it is some days for us. We go looking for trouble. We say: "This time will be different. This time I won't get drunk. This time I will control my passion. This time I won't get depressed." We reach out to pet our own chained dog and usually get bitten again. And for no good reason except that we seem fascinated by those things that can destroy us. Our sport is to tempt fate foolishly.

Oh, we are most rational and prudent when it comes to seeing the madness in the lives of others. Yet we cannot see our own madness. Thus poor old Peter was convinced that Jesus was insane when he insisted that he "had to" go up to Jerusalem to be killed. Peter could see no sense in that at all, and he told Jesus as much. Yet later on Peter could not see that he was tempting fate by putting his own terror to the test when he followed Jesus into the courtyard of the executioners. Peter's time for bravery was to come later on, but he should have known that it was not to be on the evening of Holy Thursday when he had already fallen asleep once, cut off an ear in a fit of passion, and run away with the others. He was not having a good night and he should have realized it. But he didn't, and he ended up falling before his fear, as Jesus had predicted.

However, at least he tempted fate out of love. As long as he could stand it, he just had to see what was going to happen to his beloved Jesus. In a way Peter was like Jesus. They both tempted disaster for good reasons. Jesus had a mission; Peter was in love. My days of daring are not always so reasonably explained. Too often I return to my chained dogs for no good reason at all. Thus, it is silly for me to return again and again to some affront or unkindness that is over and done with. The only place such bruises can exist now is in my mind, to fester and poison my life. Indeed, some of my chained dogs are only in my mind. They are beasts of imagination.

Others are very real. I can point to a history of failure and yet am convinced that the future will be different. How foolish! If my job made me sick yesterday, it will probably do so today. If I got into an argument with my friend about "X" yesterday, the fight will continue today if I bring up "X" again. If I got depressed alone in my room yesterday, it is not likely that today's isolation will make me feel any better.

And so it goes, as I continue to bait the mad dogs which are mine. Indeed, they are mine. They are not in some foreign land. They are in me. They *are* me. What am I to do? Perhaps pray . . .

Jesus, if today I must challenge my chained dog, let it be for a good reason. Let me not pretend that my weakness is not there. If I am to be bitten today, let the pain be mine and no one else's. If I am hurt with my eyes open and for a good reason and without injury to others, it will be easier to lick my wounds without regret and prepare humbly for tomorrow's hound.

The Silent Spirit

On some days I read with envy the story of Peter, newly baptized in the Spirit, speaking in his own language and yet being understood by people from all over the world. On that day he had the gift of tongues. On many of my days I seem to have the gift of confusion. There are days when I talk clear English to English-speakers who do not seem to understand me at all. Worse still, they seem to know that even I don't understand, perhaps because I am not truly convinced of the truth I speak.

What a gap there is between speaking, understanding, and conviction. I learned to speak as a child. (Somewhat late, I am told, much to the dismay of my parents who feared that I was an idiot. Strange it is that when I was small and quiet I was called dumb, and now that I am big and spout nonsense I am called wise.) In any case, I began to use words when I was very young. But even now, so much later on, I don't always understand, and even less frequently am I truly convinced. I have developed many nice-sounding phrases over the years but I am conquered by few of them.

It is much easier to speak than to understand. To be convinced is hardest of all. It is no trouble to say almost anything. Words are only well-formed waste wind. If I tried to keep stale air in my lungs it would kill me. Exhaled, it can become a song. To understand what I say or sing demands that I look at myself as I really am. My words are expressions of me. How I purr flows from the kind of cat I am. And sometimes it is difficult to face up to the fact that I am more of the alley variety than of those with pedigree.

I must understand myself before I can understand what I say. To say "I love you" sounds the same whenever I say it. But the meaning can vary. If I am still a selfish child the words may mean: "You are for me an object of pleasure." If I am striving to escape my solitariness the words may mean: "You are for me pleasant company." But if I am truly overcome by the goodness of my beloved my words express the highest desire of good: "I wish for you, my dearest, every good. I wish for you every happiness for eternity and without condition."

Happy indeed is a loved one who is the object of such noble words. Happier still if the one who says the words understands them and is conquered by them. To be conquered by my words means to be prepared to act on them.

My love may be a true love. It may even be the highest form of love. And yet it may be too weak to stand practice. It is easy to say "I would give my life for you" when there is no demand for action. It is easy to say "I will do anything for your good" as long as I am not faced with "anything" that is unpleasant. It takes a great love to accept the fact that I am bad for my beloved and therefore must walk away.

Words are easy; understanding is difficult; conviction may be impossible if I am unsupported in my weakness. Paul reflects this truth when he writes, "No one cay say, 'Jesus is Lord,' except in the Holy Spirit" (1 Cor 12:3). Obviously he is not referring to saying the words. He speaks of being conquered by them.

My parents need not have worried about my dumbness. The day soon came when I opened my mouth and began a career of foolish speaking. Now that I am older and educated I can share the proud claim of the clergy: "Though I sometimes may be taken for granted, I will never go without saying." In these later days I need the gift of "shut-upness." I need more times of healthy silence so that when the appropriate occasions come for saying important things like "I love you" or "Jesus is the Lord" I will be able to understand the words and be conquered by them. There are some days when the Spirit is silent in my life. These are the days when I am better off sitting quietly, turning over my life in my mind, waiting without noise for the whisper of the Spirit in my life.

Jesus, ask the Spirit to come to me with that most precious gift, the gift of silence. I need the power to keep my mouth shut until such time as I am ready to whisper of my love and proclaim my Lord with understanding and conviction.

Idiot Days

There are some days in our lives when we should have permission to be idiots, because that is exactly how we feel. I know such days are coming in my life when I get up, step on the alarm clock, shave with tooth paste and start to shower without soap. If I had any sense I would go back to bed immediately, but characteristic of the day is that I will not have any sense.

Perhaps Paul had finished such a day when he wrote: "Keep careful watch over your conduct. Do not act like fools but like thoughtful men" (Eph 5:15-20). Perhaps that's how he felt when he fell off his horse and got up a Christian, or when he was lowered in a basket to escape the fury of a town. Paul preached about wisdom but he too must have had days when he felt like an absolute idiot. Perhaps he harangued the crowd as one of my friends did, saying: "Behold, the fields are white with the harvest but the laborers are nuts." Or did he counsel the sinner (as I did) that humans should remember that they are very "feek and weeble."

On idiot days I am consoled by the book of Proverbs:

> Wisdom has built herself a house . . .
> and proclaimed from the city's heights,
> "Who is ignorant? Let him step this way" (9:1, 3-4).

There is still a chance even when I am an idiot for no good reason. Sometimes there are good reasons for a dimmed mind. There is a natural simpleness in being very young and sometimes in being very old. But there are also foolish days that we make for ourselves by our own conscious stupidity. These are the days when we drink too much bad wine and then spout spurious wisdom that is unremembered the next day. These are the days of the simple-minded romantic who repeats all the glorious love promises ever heard, without considering the seriousness of making vows that cannot be kept. Idiot days are the days of anger when we lash out at all around us and then spend the rest of the week trying to get our feet out of our mouths.

At the end of such days I thank God that I will be judged on my attempts at love rather than my wisdom. I thank Jesus-God that he did not say that I had to be a genius to be saved. Like Wisdom in the book of Proverbs, Jesus invites the simple to eat and drink from his table and says that we shall be saved if we eat and drink of him. That makes me feel a lot better. Even on my worst days I seem to be able to eat and drink. Even on my worst idiot days, when everything else seems to be going wrong, I can still have the possibility of feeding forever on that bread which is Jesus (John 6:51-58). This is true even on those terrible days when I discover that I have poured my morning coffee down the front of my shirt.

> Jesus, help me get through my days of stupidity without hurting myself or others. Keep me away from things fragile. Don't let me talk too much until my mind returns. Let me sit quietly refreshed by your grace as I grin in silliness through another idiot day.

Sharing Our Love

God made us in such a way that we are capable of loving and we need to be loved. Both Jesus-God and his friends (e.g., Paul) say that love is just fine and that we should love not only God but also other human beings. What we find out for ourselves is that being in love can be aggravating. Sometimes it is like being between everything and nothing. It has a special joy but it also has a special pain.

If I never loved I would never miss a departed love so much. Like a dead fish I would lie impassively on the surface of a still sea in the suns of my passing days, with no special feelings and therefore no special agonies, as other creatures move through the ripples of my life. If I never loved I would not realize the infinite possibilities for joy. I would not be so conscious of the limits that make it impossible for all possibilities to be realized. Our thirst for the good is infinite, but in this life at least our capacity is sadly restricted.

We cannot devour those we love as we would sometimes like to because we can never be more than part of their lives. We cannot give ourselves totally to them because they are only part of our life. Even if we have a lifetime romance, we can still clutch only part of each other's lives. The ultimate pain of being loved and loving creatures is that we always die thirsty. In this life we have never tasted enough love. There has never been anyone in this life who could give us all the loving time we wanted.

There is only one love who can give us all the love we need: Jesus-God. And this is so because he is the only one who has an eternity to waste. The mystery of Jesus-God, which we will only later come to understand, is that while he shares his love with all of us he is able to give unlimited time and love to each one of us. The Syrophoenician woman seemed to know this. She, the outsider, came to Jesus seeking a cure for her daughter. She was not put off when Jesus said, "It is not fair to take the children's bread and to cast it to dogs." Instead of going away she responded, "But, Lord, even the dogs eat of the crumbs that fall from their master's table" (Matt 15:21-28). She knew that Jesus-God's love was so great that there was plenty to go around. She knew that the emptiness of God is richer than any human fullness.

Thus it is that the most perfect love, the fullest love that we humans can have for each other, is that which passes through Jesus. We can consume each other totally by reaching out and touching each other through the fullness of Jesus. We are able to rest eternally in Jesus with our earthly love. We won't need to steal time from others anymore. And we will be happy finally in our shared love.

> Jesus, let me hold my human love embraced by you. Let me reach out to them through you. You can always be present to them while I cannot. You can always protect them while I cannot. You can always hold them and wipe away their tears while I cannot. Be kind to them always, even when I must be away busy about other things.

The "Oh Me! Oh My!" Generation

"Oh Lord, on days of feeling good deliver me from gloomy friends."

It usually happens like this: I am walking down the street feeling pretty good, not terrific perhaps but pretty good. At least I feel good enough to anticipate the day with some hope. But then it happens. I am suddenly under attack by the Blues Army. I am under attack by the "Oh Me! Oh My!" tribe, people with nothing terribly wrong with them except the passion to cry:

"Oh Me! Oh My! Life has passed me by!"
"Oh Me! Oh My! I fear that I shall die!"

To this cry of pain they add reasons suitable to the occasion:

"The sun is out, Oh Me!"
"The night is dark, Oh My!"
"I have a date, Oh Me!"
"I don't have a date, Oh My!"
"Why do I have to go to bed, Oh Me!"
"Why do I have to get up, Oh My!"
"I am growing old, Oh Me!"
"And to top it off, I am getting a cold, Oh My!"

So there I am walking down the street feeling pretty good, not terrific perhaps but pretty good, and suddenly I am covered by the woes of others. I feel rotten, or at least very guilty about feeling good.

It's nice on such days to find someone who is smiling, someone who is an instrument of cheer for me. It is just fine on such days to discover someone who loves me enough not to remind me that the world and I are going to hell. On many days I am convinced of that and need no reminding. With a cheerful, understanding, loving friend by my side I can feel cheerful on most days. I can recognize the good things in my life. For example, I can realize that I feel pretty good, not terrific perhaps but pretty good (there is that ache in my hair and the toe that itches). On most days I can look around and remember someone who cares for me. I can remember that there are those I care about very much and that they are the brightness of my life. On most days, even in New England, the weather is fairly decent, and every day I share this universe with a Jesus-God who sings to me:

Come, let us celebrate together!
Let us be cheerful in this great good world
of blue skies and pungent seas,
of crimson-gold autumns and ivory winters.
Come, let us celebrate together in this very good world
where children laugh and dance on yellow beaches
and one can sometimes find the soft gaze of love
shining in the eyes of a dear one.
Come, let us sing together
of this world which is the beginning
of your endless life with me!

Indeed, Jesus wants me to be cheerful this day. Maybe together we can fight off the attack of the blues mounted by the "Oh Me! Oh My" generation. Jesus had a laugh now and again. And he never said it was a sin to be joyful.

> Jesus, help me listen to the sorrows of others with understanding but don't let them give me the blues on days when I feel pretty good.

Days of Kindly Neglect

"Come on," they said, "let us concoct a plot against Jeremiah. The priest will not run short of instruction without him, nor the sage of advice, nor the prophet of the word. Come on, let us hit at him with his own tongue; let us listen carefully to every word he says" (Jer 18:18).

Lord, what a burden that would be some days: to be taken seriously. I couldn't stand the trial of always being listened to carefully, of having every word analyzed and measured and written down and understood and remembered and taken very, very seriously. The beauty of teaching theology or philosophy is that most of the folks are asleep before you say anything dangerous. Best of all is the trick of my friend in the tropics: turn off the microphone and turn on the fan when you don't know what you are talking about.

Oh, I know that most days I complain about being left alone, of getting no respect, of not having anyone pay any attention to me. But on some days the neglect is truly kindly. I am protected by the distraction of others when I say my frequent words that I only half understand. On such days my best friends are the deaf ones. They at least pretend not to hear the silliness that flows from my vacant mind, my petulance, my childishness, my injured humanity. And I can face them the next day.

So, please God, my dear friends will remember that I love them deeply, and won't pay me any attention on my days when I am better off alone. I'll plan to see them again tomorrow, and I hope that stupidity, like alcohol, can be slept off.

The trouble with you, Jesus, is that you have very good ears and you hear even the unspoken word hidden in the garble of pretentious sounds sometimes flowing from my big mouth. You may have to hear me, Lord, but don't always take me seriously, especially on those days when I don't know clearly who I am or where I am going.

Days of Pretending

When I was little my favorite time was Saturday morning. I would lie on the floor of our sun-dappled living room and listen to the radio program "Let's Pretend." Encouraged by the mysterious voices coming from the family Philco, a true cathedral of radios that rose majestically over my short supine frame, I would fly back and forth over space and time pretending to be just about anything I pleased. It was simply delightful.

Naturally I never pretended bad things. I was in control of my pretense. It was not at all like the terrifying dreams of night that would sometimes wake me crying. I was the master of my daytime pretending. Though much too young to understand the romance involved, I responded quickly to the distress of my Saturday morning princesses. In response to their cries I would ride to their relief. I, the ebony-armored knight with my magic sword, would rescue countless raven-haired damsels from tears and loneliness. Of course they would fall madly in love with me. They found it easy somehow to overlook the fact that I was only four feet tall and that shaving was a task to be anticipated but as yet uncalled for.

Indeed, it was delightful. I never pretended to fail. I never pretended that any lovely maiden rejected my affection with a laugh. It always was just fine on those Saturday mornings because people are always pretty and never have bad times on the children's shows. I pretended and had no guilt because I was very little and had no responsibilities. I was expected to be nothing more than I was: a short, fuzz-faced, fantasizing (and somewhat fantastic) child.

It was only much later that I discovered that pretending could devastate my spirit and injure those I love. When I was very young I could move from one week's pretense to the next without injury to myself or others. When I grew up I found out that morning pretendings always end when I'm faced with the hard reality of life. I discovered that adult pretendings at the wrong times and about the wrong things bring agony. I could not very long pretend to love without agony to the one fooled. I could not very long pretend not to love without terrible pain to myself trying to live a lie.

When we are old reality always catches us. Overindulgence in pretending, like too much to drink, brings a special pain the morning after. When I pretend to be a king or a god, when I pretend to be some superior being with no human weakness or stupidity or needs, I lose the ability to be a truly living man facing up to my own fair share of human foibles. When I try to spend every day walking the golden shore of some utopia that exists only in my imagination, I lose the chance to see the love and light that surrounds me in my real world. Oh, I must still have some days of pretending even though I am older and bigger, but it can only be some days. I cannot live my life in pretense, though there are times when I would dearly love to do so.

The difference between God and me is that he doesn't pretend in serious matters. He does not pretend about love. He does not pretend about what he wants us to do. He does not pretend about what he is and what we are. Oh, he does fool around a bit. For example, Jesus must have spent some time playing with the children. But God fools around only during play time. He is serious when he should be serious.

Thus when the Father sat down with Moses to work out the ten commandments he was not pretending when he commanded, "Do this!" But the people were pretending when they responded, "Of course we will do everything the Lord has told us" (Exod 24:3-8). They made a great fuss about obedience, going out and spilling some poor animal's blood over the altar to prove their sincerity, but it was just pretense. They couldn't wait to get on with breaking the commandments so recently delivered. They were willing to say or do anything as long as it was someone else's bull that was to be gored.

When Jesus-God came to sacrifice there was no bull. He used his own blood to prove his love. "He entered the sanctuary not with the blood of goats and calves but with his own blood" (Heb 9:12). When Jesus said that he was going to sacrifice for us, he did not pretend. He did not carry a bull to Golgotha. He went alone. So when humanity started to look around on the afternoon of Good Friday for a sacrificial animal, they found only Jesus. And they nailed him. Literally, they *nailed* him.

Again, Jesus-God was deadly serious on the evening before his death when he gave his followers his last gift, his own body and blood. The people there did not exactly understand what was going on. They were still pretending to be conquerors of the world. They could not believe that Jesus was serious when he said, "This is my Body. This is my Blood." They could not believe that he would actually die, that he was leaving and thus concerned about leaving himself with them in some different way. They were not able to understand because they were still pretending to be more than they were. They could not understand until they came back to reality, until they had run away and had come back, until they had hidden in fright, until they had cautiously touched the risen Lord. When they finally stopped pretending to be gods, they realized that their call to glory was through death, as it was for Jesus. When they stopped pretending, they were able to repeat the sacrifice of the Mass as Jesus had told them to do.

And so it is with me: Jesus-God will come to me in the reality of my life. But first I must accept that reality and not pretend that I am different from what I am. I can still pretend some times. But they must be the right times.

Jesus, help me dream beautiful things, but only at times good for pretending. Let me be serious when I should be serious. Don't let me look at my real life with regret, because I am what I am and you can love me only as I am, not as I might pretend to be.

Days of "Taking out the Garbage"

I am frightened. Jesus said that I must do God's will to get to heaven (Matt 7:21), but I don't have the time. I am so tied up doing silly things like taking out the garbage that I have no time for the wonderful tasks God wants me to do. It seems as though I am dying by bits and pieces, eaten away by jobs of no consequence. I am eaten away by jobs that could be done just as well by someone with less credentials. It seems that I am overqualified for most of the things I do. And yet I must do them because others are just too stupid or just don't care. Here I am planning my life for the next twenty years and I must stop to move the furniture. Here I am writing that perfect piece of prose and the baby cries and I must change a diaper. Here I am meditating and just about ready to touch that highest mystical plateau when I am called upon to take out the garbage.

I am shrinking away through the waste of my time. I am becoming shriveled as precious units of my force slip away. Energy that could be used to discover and write down what life is truly about is simply wasted breaking up fights among adult infants. I am diminished and feel like shouting: "God, do I have to do everything! Can't some of this junk be taken care of by someone else! Can't the garbage be taken out by someone less important than I!" Jesus-God must understand my frustration because he went through it. I bet there was an eighth cry from his cross that we never hear about. It was at the end when he raised his head and cried: *"Eloi, Eloi, Cur Mihi!* (Lord, Lord, why me!) Why couldn't this be done by a member of the staff! Do I have to do everything myself!" And he had a right to be furious, for he had been trapped into taking out other people's garbage. He was trapped into taking out my garbage.

Could it be that he wants me to do just that, take out garbage, do small things of no importance? According to Jesus-God, on the last day many who are cast away will plead: "Lord, Lord, have we not prophesied in your name? Have we not exorcised demons by its power? Did we not do many miracles in your name as well?" (Matt 7:22) And Jesus will reply: "I never knew you. Out of my sight!" (Matt 7:23)

I can imagine them saying as they fell away: "Never knew me, Lord? After all the fine things I did in casting out demons and giving prophecy? What in the world did you want of me, Lord?" Perhaps Jesus will say, "I wanted you to take out the garbage."

The possibility helps me understand. Perhaps I am meant to die in little pieces by spending my life-force doing inconsequential things with good spirit. Nothing is less consequential than anything else if Jesus wants it.

I don't feel any better. I still feel wasted as I stand here with the garbage bag broken in my hand and others' refuse all over my shoes. I feel useless in what I must do today. But maybe Jesus felt the same way on the cross and that's why he picked me out to do these wasting things. After all, misery loves company.

> Jesus, I would say more but I must go and make the beds. Excuse me. Or, better still, forgive me.

Days of Sound and Movement (Signifying Nothing)

There are days when the things that surround me seem more important than anything else. On days when no one seems to care, my things are friendly. My radio, my television and my car seem to be my best loves some days, when God seems but a word and people are busy about other people and not about me.

Of course my things cannot love me. But their lack of love does not hurt because it cannot be hoped for. The indifference of my radio or my television or my car does not make me sad. It is not at all like the indifference of all those people around me who are busy about other people but not about me.

My radio, my television, my car: they do their best. The little that they have is all mine. And just as well that it is. If they disappointed me I would throw them out. But this is something I can't do to all those people who live with me and seem so concerned about other people but not about me.

I guess it is true that on some days I make friends with my "mammon." But that is because on those days I feel cast out by my God and by all those friends who are so terribly busy about other people but not about me. Is my mammon the mammon of iniquity? Even so, at least it is mine. I can turn on my radio anytime I want to. It will talk on my command. If the voice is very sincere I can pretend that it is talking just to me, pretend that I am more important to it than all those anonymous ears that may be listening also, pretend that my little radio knows me and understands me and maybe even cares for me. When the pretense does not work, at least the disembodied sounds help me not to think about loneliness.

My television is a good friend too. Sometimes it gives me hope that worlds of beauty and laughter and answers exist. The problems it examines make mine pale by comparison, and all are solved in an hour or less (complete with commercials)! Oh, it is true that sometimes my television has bad days, bringing worlds of silliness or boredom or horror into my room. But I can turn these off; not so with the dull and painful and silly world that is my reality some days.

On such days I need my car because my car gives me the chance to be somewhere else, and thus perhaps somewhere better. The promise is exciting even though unlikely to be fulfilled. No matter where I go I always find myself there, with all my disreputable baggage. Sad to say, if my day is empty here it will be empty anywhere. I can pack my radio, pack my television, and drive off in my pretty car to any new place I choose. But without my God and without someone to care about, that place too will be nothing more than a place of empty sounds, of "sounding brass and tinkling cymbal" (1 Cor 13:1), signifying nothing.

> And so, Jesus – and so, my friend – today I will stay still for a while and wait for you to come to me. Oh, I may listen to my radio and watch my TV and polish my car, but only to pass the empty time as I wait for the warmth of my Lord and my friend who now have time for me.

On A Bench by the Sea

I sat by the sea today and wondered if just possibly heaven might be a bench under a blue sky by a quiet green sea where the air is warm and the only sounds are those of gulls feeding and ocean-ripples on a pebbled beach.

On such days by the sea my fears fade and suddenly the universe seems just fine.

There is no place for science here. It would spoil the beauty of my space by insisting that this blue-green world is just a tiny blob in a limitless universe, a void where there are no sounds because there is nothing at all to carry the waves nor are there any ears to hear.

But indeed the truth must be faced. As I enjoy the moment with its bright sky and gentle sea I am sitting in a tiny cocoon of reflected light, light that has traveled without blinking or thinking through path-less unaffected darkness. It is only this tiny spot made for me that reflects cold light with glory.

And so as I sit for a moment in the midst of infinity I am conscious that I am touched with special love. God made me for no good reason. He cares for me with very little reason. How else can I explain that he made my sky blue rather than ugly brown? How else can I explain an ocean that is brilliant green when it could so easily have been gray? How else can I explain that I have eyes to see the colors and ears to hear the sounds?

Indeed, I am loved. And the thought makes me warm.

Jesus, sit and be happy with me for a while on this grand day you have made.

"The Trinity Lives in Us, My Friend!"

When I was little I was always struck by the brevity of the Mass on Trinity Sunday. It seemed as though I were being told: "Well, here it is, the TRINITY! Look at it and love it but don't say too much because you probably will make a mistake." Later on in theology the picture was filled out some more by the slightly absurd attempt to give job descriptions to the three persons. The Father created, the Son saved, the Spirit loved, and all was fine with the world. As before, the day of Trinity passed quickly, but now it left behind a sense of satisfaction. God seemed to use energy efficiently and was in control of things. It was a fine day, but one dedicated more to thinking about the mystery than doing anything about it. This was before I understood that the Trinity is not only "out there" somewhere; it is here, my friend, and we poor humans in some way perform its functions for each other. We help each other know that the Trinity lives in us every day.

In some strange way my dear friends create me. In some way they make me what I am. Their being here has called forth feelings un-tapped by any other. They make me live in a special way. They have become part of my reason for living.

They have sacrificed themselves for me. They have given me attention, particles of their precious time. Just as Jesus "emptied himself" to become human for them and for me, they become part of me by spending part of their life on me.

They have touched me with the spirit of love and I speak in tongues, uttering strange songs like these about life and love and death. They make me hum great truths only partially understood by this minstrel.

Through our love for each other we bring alive the mad mystery of God. Through a strange human circumincession they are in my life and I am in theirs. I touch them even in these words they can read. I can and must show them today how God sees them: precious, beloved, never to be duplicated. In the love of my friends, I can come to believe that I am worthy of love. I must try to hold them as God holds them always, surrounded by love. Together we are surrounded by the Trinity.

Every day we must show the Trinity to each other and make the works of this triune God live in us: the artistry of the Father, as we create light and order in each other's solitary chaotic darkness; the companionship of the Son, as we are with each other in good times and in bad; the passion of the Spirit, as we touch each other with the fire of love.

The Father made me man. But my friends have been a part of making me "Donald," this person who has learned of God through knowing them.

Jesus, I thank you for my dear friends. Through such human love I can understand why you and the Father and the Spirit made the world. Once experienced, love must be extended to others.

3   Autumn Days

The Christian liturgy has no special color for growing old, but nature does. During autumn in New England we can see them, the violent reds and golds of old leaves reflecting rays of a full sun beginning to lower on the horizon. As my days lengthen they imitate such splendor, the glory of leaves that are not so much dying as passing to new life. In their glory the leaves of autumn seem like the spring foliage of a new life to come. They seem to be passing out of the darkness of this world's womb in a blaze of glory, already touched by that new sun of eternity.

My days are painted with such colors, the colors of a mature and fruitful life. It is an advent of sorts. I am moving to new things. But now the colors of my expectation are not the vague gray of the wombed infant. I don't have a misty hope for glory as yet unannounced. If I have been lucky in life so far I will have experienced the presence of Jesus. In my waning years I shall thus know that I am held by Jesus-God. It is for this reason that my autumn waiting is lightened by the glory of the sun. The colors of my autumn are the royal colors of Christ the King living in me.

There is no clear sign of the beginning of my autumn days, but there are hints. I begin to notice that many my age have a tendency to get sick and die. I spend more time celebrating anniversaries and going to reunions, strange celebrations where I look around with unconscionable glee at the havoc wrought by the ravages of time on the other members of my class. As I grow older there are signs of increasing impatience as I realize that time is measured out sparingly and can easily be wasted.

The days can be rich and full. Love has usually matured. The agony of the young romantic is finally over. We realize that love has lasted and that we can fulfill its modest demands. We accept our loves as they are. Passion is still present but now we feel comfortable with our love. We not only rejoice in our embraces. We are secure in each other's arms. We are able to be at rest together. Fortunate are we to have this blooming of love during our autumn days. We cannot have it earlier because it takes much patience and waiting. Without such love the days of our autumn easily become cold and gray and empty.

Autumn days are not simply times of waiting. These are times for new passions, new ambitions. Prudence is mistakenly identified as a mature virtue. Far from it! Waiting is a game for the young. They have time. When my leaves begin to fall I feel a panic to get on with life, to get things done, to experience that one great love hidden for so many years in my heart. I must take that one great autumn voyage before the winter winds make great new adventures impossible. I want to avoid as long as possible those days of failing when my ardor for this world's loves cools and I begin to reach out absently with mind-fingers to some unknown future world.

And thus it is that in autumn I clutch my loves and my tasks more tightly. I fear to retire for that may mean that I will have nothing more to do. I fear the loss of my dear friend because that may mean that I am destined to face winter alone. I try to hide my lengthening days even from myself. I claim to be in my prime as I preen and pamper the dulling shades of my dying body. But all around me the leaves are falling and I begin to accept the fact that I have not here a lasting city. I am well advised to get on with singing songs yet unsung, kissing loves yet unwooed, and preparing for Jesus-God, that one certain companion through the days that lie ahead.

Happiness in Autumn

It can be dangerous to think too much. Once, after what seemed to me to be an absolutely inspiring lecture on happiness, one of my students remarked that she had been perfectly happy until she began thinking about it. Of course the definition of happiness would not tend to promote glee. One's joy could very easily be dampened by the dry reminder that one is experiencing "the conscious satisfaction of an innate appetite." Thinking about the definition could lead to wondering guiltily whether all one's appetites were in fact natural, or speculating about whether being conscious of some was a curse or blessing. Perhaps my student was right — that dumbness and happiness go together. After all, we do speak of people being "happy as clams" and clams are not noted for skills in reflection.

But "happy clams" do remind us that happiness is relative. Perhaps the only reason we say a clam is happy is that it smiles when its mouth is shut (quite different from some of us who are happy only when our mouths are open and operating). But now that you think about it, the clam should be happy. It does not have too many innate appetites to satisfy. The clam does not and cannot want very much. The clam does not worry about what it does not have. Indeed, it hardly thinks at all. My student would have been delighted to be a clam, or so she said. But I suspect that after a while her position would have worn on her. To equate happiness with unconsciousness seems a bit odd. I may feel poorly as I write these thoughts, but to say that the rock I sit on is happier by far seems absurd, even taking into consideration the noble burden it temporarily carries. Happiness is not rooted in not knowing what one is missing. Its essence is a conscious possession of what one truly needs.

Since happiness depends on some intelligent discrimination, I suspect that the happiest times are those somewhat later on in life. As we lose our teeth and grow in wisdom there is a greater chance that we will begin to share the look and happiness of the proverbial clam. We humans (like those clams) have certain shared hungers. We cannot choose not to have them; we can only choose to accept them. But to accept them intelligently we must also be willing to accept the limits on their satisfaction dictated by our state in life. We all want to live and to love and to have our lives mean something, but the way in which these needs are satisfied are unique for each one. Indeed even in the individual there are different ways of filling these hungers at different stages of life.

When we are very young there is a chance that we will feel the fullness of physical life. When I was a child it seemed that I could run and dance forever. There was no need to save strength for a rainy day. While playing on the beach on a Jersey summer's day there were no rainy futures. There was only that moment when I was part of an exciting environment of sand, sea, and sky. The perception of being alive dominated. I was aware of being cared for (there was always someone to tell me to come home on time) but I did not moon over it. I did not fret over whether I was worthy of love. Nor did I fear to lose it. The love of my family for me was simply an expected fact of life. I suppose I loved them, but being so young I could not identify the feeling. I shared the natural egoism of the baby, believing that the whole world owed me love, and not understanding when others did not have the time or desire to fulfill my desires (a not uncommon occurrence for the youngest of seven). In those very early years I was closer to the consciousness of the clam than of the wise man, but I did not share the clam's reticence. I yelled a lot when no one paid attention because that to me was the only sign of love and my importance that I could recognize.

As I grew older there still was an awareness of full physical life. But now I became more conscious of how I looked. More consciously I sought love and was convinced that to be lovable I somehow had to look good. More consciously I began to give my love to others, often without their knowing it. In this time of adolescent anonymous loving I gave my affection to movie stars, girls on the block, ladies on the subway, pining away with an infinite affection for beloved(s) who never knew I existed. I hoped that others might love me but was distressed when they did not manifest their love by giving me my own way. I couldn't stand any rejection, perhaps because I was already convinced that I was a rotten kid and needed no confirmation from the indifference of others. With all of this I had the special happiness of youth. I was full of life; I was becoming more and more free; I had hope. My life was not in jeopardy and there seemed to be an infinity of chances of love and meaning before me.

I am more secure in my happiness now in my autumn years. Now I can look back on days of accomplished love and meaning. I have learned my limitations. One of the peculiar joys of autumn days is the deadening of the temptation to look into other pastures for supposedly greener grass. I have learned in talking to friends about life and death and love that every field has its ruts. Believing in Providence I come to the conclusion that the love of God has directed me to the place I am because that just happens to be the best place for me. My life has been fitted to me by the Father just as my baby pajama-suit was fitted to me by a loving mother. My life is somewhat solitary and reflective and my baby pajama-suit had big feet and small arms because that was the most comfortable fit for me. Aggravations are not the sign of being in the wrong place. There is just too much starch from time to time.

In autumn years we understand that our thirst for love and meaning is not satisfied without failures. Any amazing fulfillment comes only after some false starts in life's maze. We understand that our happiness is fitted to us. It is special to us. We cannot be any happier by trying to be somebody else. We are where we are because of a lifetime of fulfilling desires that flow directly from our special gifts and needs. We would be in an unholy mess elsewhere. The fact that I am a priest by vocation and a philosopher by profession is God's great gift to the married state and the profession of brain surgery. Most priests I know (including myself) would make strange husbands/fathers, and it is a well-known fact that it is dangerous to give a knife to a philosopher.

In my autumn years I can perceive the happiness that I have: the life that has been given to me, the mystery of love I have shared, the work I have been able to do. I need not envy the life of anyone else. God has been good in bringing me to this point. My happiness is not perfect. But probably it never will be. That is why eternity will always be interesting, finding new ways of expressing my life to my divine and human loves. And God will find it interesting too, because I will continue to express my life and his glory in my own unique (if not positively odd) way.

Jesus, I thank you for the years that have been mine, the love that I have given and received, the tasks I have been able to do. All told, it has not been too bad, even with my hiatal hernia. (But nobody's perfect, except you).

On Being Fifty

The first peculiarity of beginning the sixth decade of life is the passion to say something about it before living it, a quirk not common to those still drinking the delightful wine of youth.

At fifty we can no longer fool ourselves into believing that there is still lots of time. The odds are that our life is half over when we become fifty, unless we are tortoises. When we are twenty we don't think about odds at all. At thirty we are too worried about not being twenty to look ahead. At forty (with all our aches) we can still claim that life is just beginning. At fifty all pretense ends. We may claim to be entering the "golden years" but we must realize that the tinge of gold comes from the weakening rays of a dying sun. We begin to wonder: "Is it too late? Is it too late to do something of importance? Is it too late to love and be loved? Can a person be lovable on the sunset side of the hill?"

The curse of the sixth decade of life is impatience. We think, "Woe to one who wastes my time, who steals the precious minutes trickling from my diminished years!" We grasp at time and then oddly enough, when it is given, we sit and dream and write down words like these about life half done with such a small history of tiny tasks imperfectly accomplished.

But with all of that I must confess to being warmed at fifty. I remember all those who seem to care for me, all those who have put up with me kindly as I passed through my various moods, my crazy thirst for love, my itch to get on with things. At fifty I remember those I love and I am calmed. I remember that I have seen Jesus in the lives of others and I am able to hope.

The cards I receive tell me that I am remembered. The mystery of my place in the minds and hearts of others promises that I shall never be alone, though a solitary I may be. I live now not alone but in the hearts of my friends. And in our love Jesus lives and is present at this season and every season of our lives.

> Jesus, here I am "fifty and counting"! You never made it this far yourself. You rushed off to meet the Father in your early middle age. Maybe the reason I lasted this long is that I haven't done much of importance. But in any case, there is no use worrying about that! I pray only that I will have the courage to do what you ask of me in the days ahead. Don't let me lose sight of you in the lengthening shadows of my late afternoon.

Suffering

One of the hardest days in a human life is the day spent by the bed of a suffering friend, trying to make sense of it. Perhaps it is wrong to try. After all, to say that Jesus accepted suffering out of love is only to say that he chose to be human out of love. Suffering followed inevitably upon that choice. To say that Jesus wants us to suffer is simply obscene. He wants *us*, but in order to make us he had to make us limited and therefore prone to destruction. Then we messed up the situation even more by trying to pretend that we were not limited and were thereupon forced to pay the price of presumption.

Suffering has no explanation if by that we mean a purpose built into it. Suffering is an effect. It is not a cause. It is the inevitable result of my being limited and being so foolish that I cannot even reach the perfection my limits allow. Suffering is the result of the wish to drink infinite life while being a small bucket not yet filled with the modest quantity of infinite life possible to me.

The human condition is a fragile tension between anabolism and catabolism, a building up and breaking down, where the breaking down dominates most of the time. We grow in strength for eighteen odd years and fall apart for the rest of our earthly lives. We are limited by nature and weakened by primordial choice. The result is the possibility of pain. Even though our passage through life may be gentle, we are still distressed by the fear that it will not be so. Part of suffering resides in the unhappy fact that though we are limited in knowledge we have an infinite capacity for remembering and imagining. We cannot forget the past agony of ourselves and our loved ones. Our imagination seems to grasp all the worst of these torments, mix them together in a senseless stew, and present it as an assured prediction of our future history.

Thus it is that we fear physical pain even in its absence, and the fear quickly becomes the object feared. As Simone Weil noted, physical pain, or the fear of it, is always at the root of our affliction because it cannot be ignored or accepted by even the strongest spirit. Indeed, "it makes a slave of our Spirit" (*Waiting for God,* Harper Colophon Books, 1973, p. 118). And like the slave we are solitary.

Pain is personal. It cannot be shared. Like death it must be faced alone. Even the best-intentioned friend cannot take up our cross. Perhaps that's why Jesus was careful to specify that we must take up *our* cross and follow him. We can't take up his. Indeed, he can't take up ours. He can't tell us in the midst of our suffering that it really doesn't matter. Nor would it have made sense for anyone on Calvary to have tried to console him by saying, "That's O.K.! You will get over it." When we suffer, the pain exists and it is peculiarly ours. Jesus can do no more for us (assuming he doesn't simply make us well) than Simon did for him. Simon was with Jesus when Jesus was in pain. He was able to do little more. Perhaps he did relieve some of the weight of the cross and thus lessen the tearing of Jesus' shoulder. But he could not take a piece of the pain that was left and say, "This now is mine." Because it wasn't and never could be. Jesus' agony was his own and no one else's. And so too is ours. The isolation of such physical distress is feared as much as the pain.

The isolation is magnified by the very human tendency of people to avoid us when we are suffering. Friends may visit and speak to each other over our bed of pain, letting us listen in as they carry on with life, but many are quick to leave. We are angry and sad but we too avoided the dying and suffering when we had the chance. In our strength we were just like every other human being. We hated to be reminded of our future decay. None of us likes to die. We hope that at least we will die in peace. Visiting the suffering reminds us that death could very well come that way to us. We fear that distress in dying that would make of our passage the exit of a whimpering confused animal.

Thus, at the first visit of pain we cry to Christ and wait for the only response that we will accept: the end of pain. It is not enough to be told that he is with us through our suffering. In affliction the presence of God sometimes doesn't seem as precious as drawing the next breath without pain. On rare occasions a miracle occurs and suffering ceases. It does not happen very often. Indeed, it did not even happen in the garden of Gethsemani when Jesus cried in agony to a silent Father and sought the company of understanding friends only to find them sleeping someplace else. Was Jesus' suffering willed by the Father? Yes, I guess it was, but only in the sense that he wills that this world of fragile finite things should totter on.

It is very human to suffer. It is just as human not to desire it. Indeed such a desire approaches presumption, as though I could handle suffering better than Jesus and the rest of the human family could. It is true that sometimes as we stand by the bedside of a suffering loved one we cry out to take their pain and make it our own. But we do this not because we want to suffer but because we want our loved one to be at peace.

To want suffering for its own sake is inhuman and un-Christian. Better by far to share that great good will of God that we all be happy together forever in a heaven without pain. The only joy in suffering is in the realization that it is a sign of the shedding of the wounded finite character that stands in the way of our perfect happiness in God. But mostly the best we can manage is just the effort to get through.

> Jesus, help me be happy when I feel fine and not worry about future pain. When suffering comes let it be quick, and be with me to hold me during the pain. Or better still, let me slip into your arms with no suffering at all. After all, if you cried out on seeing your cross, what can be expected of a poor thing like me?

Christmas in Autumn

Jesus comes at every season of life and for every season there is a message. He comes even in the autumn of life. And thus it is that the psalmist encourages us to trust in God and rejoice, for he shall protect us from the pestilence of the night and the "noon-day devil" (Ps 90:6). It is somewhat consoling to me as I grow in age (if not in wisdom) that the middle-aged "blahs" are not special to my generation. Medieval writers used the figure of the "noon-day devil" to symbolize the special trials and tribulations of the middle years in a person's life. God exists for the middle-aged.

This assurance is important because the despair in the middle years is much more conscious than in earlier years. The sources of such hopelessness may seem trivial to those outside but for the one undergoing them they are anything but. They can paralyze one's life. This *dis-ease* of middle life comes in various forms. For a parent it may be the sadness of a breakdown in communication with children, a feeling that one has somehow failed as a parent. For the worker it may come as a realization that advancement is unlikely, that a career has come to a halt and that the future will be nothing more than a grinding out of days till retirement. For the middle-aged bachelor it may be the awareness that he is no longer a Don Juan (only a wan Don), that his chest has fallen forever below his belt and that his head is growing through his hair. For the maiden of advancing years it can come with the acceptance of the fact that she will never be twenty again.

In all its forms the "noon-day devil" convinces us that we have lost love, or at least what we have mistakenly come to believe are the conditions for love. We look into our morning mirror and see that the bloom of youth has gone down the sink. Sadly we wonder, "Who could love such an ugly thing like me?" We lump ourselves into our chair of evening, understanding that we will never be very important. Perhaps that day some "kid" made a sarcastic remark about us, or the boss (our supposed friend) kept us "cooling our heels" in the outer office while he took care of more important business. We sit there morosely and ask ourselves, "Who could love such a useless thing like me?" A spiritual desolation overcomes us. We become infected with accidie, a listlessness in the face of any spiritual challenge. We are too tired to espouse any new great cause. The old days and the old gods have gone. "Just leave me alone!" we say. "God is dead and I am dead-tired. I am no longer pretty. No one cares for me. My life has peaked on an anthill." We die though still alive.

It is a sad state, to be sure, and sadder still because it is so foolish. If there is a "noon-day devil" there is also a mid-life Christ. The same psalm that warns of the problems of middle age contains a song of joy.

Fill us at daybreak with your kindness,
    that we may shout for joy and gladness all our days.
Make us glad, for the days when you afflicted us,
    for the years when we saw evil.
Let your work be seen by your servants
    and your glory by their children:
And may the gracious care of the Lord our God be ours;
    prosper the work of our hands for us! (Ps 90:14-17)

Jesus, come to me in a special way during my middle years. Get me moving! There is still a lot to see, many to love, much work to be done. Don't let me give up on you or myself just because this old body is becoming worn. My soul continues to grow and becomes younger year by year by sharing your life. Let me remember that you didn't do your big task till after thirty. Let me stop moping and get on with my life!

Days After Great Events

How quickly great events seem to pass through my life! I forget birthdays and deathdays easily unless I write them down. My appointment book is a record of ordinary days. Most of its pages are blank, marred only by infrequent parties celebrating past great events. Most days are like Easter Monday, days of ordinary things with a few seconds here and there to reflect on past wonders, days of God's death and humans' salvation, days of empty graves and risen saviors.

Easter Monday is like every other Monday. There is the weekend waste to be carted out, carefully contained in individual bags that remind me of the Monday-people rushing off to their solitary work and worry. Somehow it seems harder to be a Christian on days after great events. Easter Monday faith is as difficult as that of Good Friday. How can anyone believe in anything extraordinary on Monday mornings? It seems easier to long for a dead God in Good Friday's dusk than to be excited about anything in this life or the next in the dull light of a usual

Monday dawn. On such mornings Jesus is neither a dramatically dying God nor brightly risen Savior. He is just there. He is like a sleepy lover smiling foggily across a dawn-dappled kitchen. He is a comforting usual presence, not solving problems or fulfilling wishes, but merely being present with us in the ordinary joys and sorrows of that day.

Is it possible to rejoice in such an ordinary presence? I believe so, for I know it is possible for us to be in love and to have that love grow through a lifetime. It is possible for me to become used to the one I love so that we become like two old shoes comfortable in being together even though we are far from being exactly the same or, for that matter, even a very good match.

Perhaps that's why Jesus rejoices when we fall in love. He knows that in the fullness of settled, comfortable human love we can become accustomed to the delight of a quiet God present on days after great events. It is important for us and for Jesus that we come to that realization. Jesus wants to be part of my life on all days, even on Easter Monday and all the other dull Mondays of my life.

> Jesus, as far as we know there was only one morning when you rose bright and shining. Most of your days began quietly. Be with me on my days when nothing much seems to happen. It would be a shame to weather days of crisis only to lose you in the dull boredom of my Monday mornings.

Talking (Carefully) to the Lord

There are some days when I am just plain scared of God. It may be that I am feeling guilty about something, like a kid who just broke the living room window. Or it may just be that on this day I feel as small as I really am in this huge universe. But for whatever reason my attitude is such that if God came for a visit I would make tracks in the opposite direction. The speed of light would be nothing compared to the speed of my fright. God for me on such days is like the man in Jim Croce's ballad: seven-foot Leroy Brown, called by the ladies "Tree" and by the gentlemen "Sir." If asked, "How do you call an infinite God?" I respond, "Very carefully!"

Like most humans I am afraid of strangers who are bigger than I am. They are strong enough to destroy me and, as far as I know, they might just have such an inclination. I know that God is big. And on some days he seems like a stranger. So I don't fool with him. I feel like the disciples running to Jesus asking how they should pray to God. (Imagine their surprise later on when they realized that *he* was God!) How to pray to God! You can almost taste their fright:

> If I am going to call up God I just better be careful! I just better know *exactly* what I am going to say, because I am talking to *God!* And if I approach him in the wrong way he may get mad like the tired policeman who catches me breaking the law and puts me in jail, or like the boss with indigestion who catches me "goofing off" and fires me, or like the nasty teacher who thinks I'm stupid and fails me!

Indeed I can understand the disciples when they said to each other: "We must be careful when we speak to God. We must know the rules. So let's ask Jesus (good old Jesus) how we should pray." And they did. And Jesus told them to say these words to God:

> Hello, Father, I hope that today is good for you and that tomorrow will be fine too. Help me today to get the things I need to live. Forgive me today if I have saddened you as I today forgive those who have saddened me. Above all, protect me because I am little and am often afraid.

It must have taken the disciples a little while before they were able to say "Our Father" to God. Even now there are some dark days when I can't say it. God is my father? It seems too good to be true.

> Jesus, on my scared days help me not be scared of God. If I believe in him with confidence I can bear any fright that this world brings. Without such trust any day can become fearsome.

Days of Being Bound

Jesus said to Peter: "When you were young you girded yourself and walked where you wished. But when you are old you will stretch forth your hands and another will gird you and lead you where you wish not" (John 21:18). The reference supposedly is to Peter's eventual execution but the words could just as well apply to any human in the autumn of life, even me. Now there seem to be few moments of absolute freedom in my life. Perhaps there are none, only some that are less *un*free.

When I was young I thought I was free to do almost anything. But even then it was not the case. Even then I was hemmed in, "girded," if you will, by limited ability and lack of daring and the vagaries of opportunity presented to me. I was not bound down by my present obligations. When I was young few were affected by my decisions to do this or that, to be thus and so. Few depended upon me and I was more free to move about without worry.

As I grew older I became more bound up. I reached a point where I was carried along by the tide of events. I became locked in by loves who have legitimate expectations of me. I have been broadened and narrowed by my history. Others "gird me and lead me where I (sometimes) wish not."

Of course it is not too bad to be tied down if the bonds are pleasant. An embrace can be just as capturing as a jail. What makes it captivating is the pleasure of the imprisonment. There is a pleasing security in being tied to a definite place in the lives of others. The chains of love are not distressing because they usually do not rub the wrong way. They can be aggravating because they do prevent us from quick changes of direction. The patience of our autumn days is sometimes merely the lack of energy to fight the bonds that gird us.

Jesus was kind in binding up Peter in his later days. He prevented him from getting lost. And so too I am lucky in the autumn of my life if the Providence of God has bound me in place, hemmed in by those who have grown to care for me. With such soft, loving bonds it will be difficult for me to wander off and make an old fool of myself.

> Jesus, thank you for my history by which you have bound me to yourself. If you can't now prevent the temptation to wander away, at least tire me out through my daily obligations so that I won't have the energy to fight the soft bonds with which you gird me.

Autumn Fire

The other day, despite my being in the autumn of my life, I felt the flash of love and I was suddenly on fire. I was hesitant and afraid because any fire is uneasily tamed and autumn fires are especially dangerous. There is so much waste accumulated in old structures and autumn fires are mostly indoors. They are not like the summer blazes that live outdoors. They shoot up quickly and are quickly gone. Any scars are greened over by abundant new growth. Not so in our autumn days. Any fire must be nurtured inside. We are jealous of any escaping warmth lest we be cold and lonely in the face of winter's blasts. Once weakened, an autumn fire is with difficulty revived. Once finally gone, it augurs death.

And thus the other day I welcomed my new autumn passion but was careful not to give into the temptation to be selfish with it, to act as though it were the only thing that existed. That would be dangerous. We old houses need clean flues so that our passions can rise to heaven. Closed in upon itself an autumn fire creates noxious fumes that can kill the innocents that dance before it. Closed in upon itself it can explode and kill the kindler and destroy the house.

It is no use admonishing old houses to have better sense than to accept new loves. I can testify that to reject such fire is easier said than done. Indeed so delightful is the new warmth that some of us almost lose control. We try to dance on our tottering foundations and in the process disturb the bats in our belfries. Each winter old houses rejoice when they learn that they can still contain fire. Any warm blaze is a great event for an old house. Not so in those sterile new condominiums, so slick and shiny, housing strangers and transients, indifferently switching warmth on and off at the touch of a button. Their fire is too automatic to be interesting. How different it is for us old mansions who need loving, careful attention if our cold bricks are ever to hold heat again!

Well, the other day this old house found fire amidst his piled ashes and the experience brought joy. The fire was warm and bright and somewhat mad, like any self-respecting flame. But it was controlled and tamed and brought light to me and those who surround me. What it shall be remains to be seen but right now it is warm and comforting. I must believe that Jesus had a hand in it. He brought fire to the earth. Pray God my fire will last.

Jesus, help me nourish the fires of my autumn days
so that they may warm me and those I love and bring
us safely home to you.

Helpless to Help

Today I discovered the special agony of the human being in love. It is to have an infinite desire to help and to realize that one's powers are finite. It is to wish all good to one's dear friend and be powerless to bring it about. It is a maddening divine thirst, a desire to say just once with effect the promise of God: "I shall wipe away every tear from your eye" (Rev 21:4). But all one can cry are the sad words of one who is helpless to help: "I can't save you, my beloved, and I weep!"

The ultimate sense of failure for human love is to see the beloved hungry, confused, sorrowing, and yet be unable to provide food or conviction or consolation. The source of ultimate despair for human love is to look into the future and to realize that despite every effort to the contrary the beloved may end hungry and alone in dingy rooms of uncaring cities. We are in terror knowing that our beloved could end up trapped in the frightening confusion of a dying mind in the corner of a state asylum.

In anticipation of unknown illnesses we cry out in our heart, "Take *my* strength, take *my* health," fearful that someday we must stand by the bed of a hopelessly ill dear friend and know that there is nothing we can do. "I could not preserve my mother's mind!" "I could not take away my sister's illness!" "I could not bring my beloved the happiness of love!" "I could not stop the kids from destroying themselves!" These cries and many others are the cries of human helplessness.

And believing in Jesus doesn't help. Indeed, *being* Jesus did not help. How else to explain the days he had? He was helpless in preventing Joseph from dying. He was helpless in avoiding his widowed mother's pain when he left her. He was helpless in making anyone love him exclusively. He was helpless in overcoming the confusion of his followers. He cured the sick but he could not force faith on them. He made the lame to walk and they walked away. He made the dumb to speak and they cursed him. He gave his closest friends his body and

blood and they abandoned him. Finally he died with his last prayer un-
fulfilled: "Father, if possible, let this cup pass from me!" (Luke 22:42)

On this day in the autumn of my life I learned that my dear friend
may be sick. Cold fingers grip my heart, because I know I can do
nothing about it.

> Jesus, take my beloved in your arms. You under-
> stand what human suffering is. You understand the
> sense of helplessness of those who must watch. Be
> with us now, for we need you in our day of weakness
> when we are helpless to help.

A Loved One's Illness

It is easier to be sick oneself than to watch the illness of a loved one,
helpless to do anything about it. There is no use pretending that the
sole cause of our distress is the pain of the other. There is a healthy
dab of self-interest in our panic. To be sure we are upset because our
friend is not feeling well. When we truly love others their joy becomes
our joy; their pain becomes our pain. They are truly part of us and we
share their life. But we cannot share their death and that is why we
tremble. If they move on, we shall be left alone. Though we may rejoice that they are moving on to a new life without pain, we cry for
ourselves because all we can see in our future is the same old painful
future now to be lived without the dear ones who made it somewhat
bearable.

Thus it is that when dear friends get sick we worry about what will
happen to them and we worry about what will certainly happen to us if
they don't recover. From the very beginning of the illness we taste the
terrible vacuum, the gap in our life, that would be left by their death.
Love does not cease with death. Love continues through death and
creates a special pain of loss. This agony of absence is the dark side of
that coin of love which brings such ecstasy when a dear friend is with
us.

I am reminded of this sometimes when I hear the rustling leaves of
late summer. They are healthy and yet they seem to tremble. Could it

be that they perceive the gradual fading of some of their fellows? In these late days of life's summer, when the first of our friends begin to depart, we the survivors tremble. It is a difficult time, these days when we still feel the vigor of life in our bodies but witness the sudden weakening of those to whom we have committed our affection.

It is more difficult than later on when we all move on together. Then at least we are not alone as we join other leaves of our vintage in the hustle and bustle of returning to the earth after a full life lived out together. There is no weeping on those cold, crisp October days when all the leaves dressed in their glorious traveling clothes fall like multi-colored snow to embrace the earth. It is autumn. They have had a good life together. And now they move arm in arm to a new ex-perience. One can almost hear them singing.

Dying is not too bad when one has company. Living can be hell when one is alone.

> Jesus, I know you are always with me and I shouldn't be lonely. But let's face it! You made me human and gave me other humans to love and be with. Don't let them get sick and leave me. I know we must all go sometime. But later, let it be later, when we can all go together to meet you on the other side of winter's darkness.

Remembering

One of the signs of the autumn of my life is a tendency to spend as much time in remembering loved ones who are dead as in enjoying loved ones who are still with me. Today is the anniversary of a dear one's death, my sister Alice, and my cry is that of anyone who has lost a loved one: "How can I reach her now?"

So much of human "missing" is tied in with a need to "touch" the beloved. Such phrases as "You live always in my heart!" are only par-tially satisfying. I want to touch my beloved again, with my eyes and ears and fingers. I want to see the dark shine of her hair, hear her laughter, feel the softness of her hand. I don't want to remember her! I want to reach out and *do something* for her. I want to affect her, to know that I am bringing good to her, to contribute to her happiness wherever she may be. I want to reach out and touch her and make her happy.

Will Jesus help me? I pray he will, because she helped me believe in him. Perhaps through my Mass I can pass through space and time and touch her. Perhaps through my Mass I can speak to her and say those things I was not able to say when she was so sick, those things I was not able to say because I was not strong enough to stand her pain.

Perhaps through Jesus' sacrifice here on the altar before me I can reach out and touch her cool forehead as I did once before when she was sleeping her way finally into death.

It should not be too hard. After all, Jesus touched me when he died, even though I was not yet born. Perhaps it is not too much to ask that through his Body and Blood I be permitted to reach through her grave and touch Alice and make her happy.

Scripture says that it is a good thing to remember the dead (2 Macc 12:46). It would be even better if I could reach out and touch my beloved through this Mass.

> Jesus, you are the only one who can truly "do good" for my dead loved ones now. Will you tell them that I care for them? Will you hold them for a minute in my name? That will make up for the times I should have held them in this life and did not.

Days of Tiredness

Some days I am not that good at being a man or in running after Jesus. I hesitate in giving my human love to dear friends and am inconstant in my race to catch up with the Lord. On some days I can just barely see him far ahead and I rush to keep up. On other days I even forget to look for him.

It seems as though my friends and I are on a long dusty path with Jesus way up there in front, just barely seen. My human loves seem more real because they are close. Jesus seems so far away sometimes.

The embrace of my dear friends gives me strength to keep running with them. They carry me with their love. I am embarrassed when they think that I know the way to Jesus and that I will carry them. They do not know that on some days all I can do is cry out in fear in the arms of their love. Just like any other man I am frightened that someday I will give up and stop running, and drag those I love down on the dusty path with me, far from Jesus.

It is hard to be a father or a king or a prophet on days when I feel like a tired little child. People ask for answers to eternal questions and all I want is to find a mother's breast on which to rest.

On some days it would be so easy to "pack it in" and stop running, to rest a while with human loves far from Jesus up ahead. Jesus seems always on the move and some days I'm too tired to keep up.

I wonder if the story of the Good Shepherd is really true? Will he come back for us, me and my dear friends? Will he lift us up and carry us in his strong arms when we fall asleep on the dusty road far behind him?

> Jesus, carry me and my human loves on our days
> of tiredness, when it seems impossible to run very fast
> after you.

Need for a Good Cure

When I get sick on the days of autumn there seems to be a fearsome usualness about it. In the days of autumn it is not a question of whether I shall catch this year's flu. It is only a question of when. Thus in autumn one can always stand a good cure. The story in Mark 1:29-39, about the time they brought the sick to Jesus, becomes moving. There must have been quite a crowd. Mark says that they brought him all who were ill and those possessed by demons and that before long the whole town was gathered outside the door.

I wonder where the end of that line is now. I don't feel so hot myself. Today I can easily echo suffering Job:

> I have been assigned months of misery.
> I have been told off on troubled nights . . .
>   and I drag through the evening restless and alone.

> My days pass swifter than a weaver's shuttle
>   and they end up with no hope.
>   I shall not see happiness again.

Worst of all, I think I am catching another cold.

Nobody enjoys being sick. Indeed, few of us even like being near the sick. Those who go to hospitals for fun are definitely strange — people who themselves may be infectious. We all visit the sick at some time or other and we feel sorry for them. But at the same time we guiltily feel joy that we are not where they are. One of the great ecstasies is the feeling we have when we walk *out* of a hospital.

Indeed, we visit the sick but we don't enjoy it. We would much prefer that all of us could be well together. We want to be healthy first of all, and then we don't want to be reminded by others' infirmities that our health is not likely to last. Even though today I feel pretty good I don't like to be reminded that even now there can be heard the "Chomp! Chomp! Chomp!" of time's terrible teeth merrily nibbling at my extremities. During autumn days there can be heard the terrified cries of the "Geritol Generation" as they watch themselves slowly falling away:

> "My God! My hair is falling!"
> "My gums are loose!"
> "My feet are curling back upon themselves!"

No matter how good I feel today I am still "slip-sliding" away.

It is no wonder that the crowds came when Jesus arrived with his medicines. I suspect that a majority were "long in the tooth" and thus ready to accept actual or potential illness as a fact of their autumn days. In their view (and mine) any day is a good day for a cure because we all are always sick or on the verge of it. Jesus came and said, "Be cured! Be saved!" and the people laughed because they knew they were sick and tired and afraid. How disappointing for them if Jesus had simply patted them on the head and said, "Why, you are just fine! You don't need a cure at all!"

If he had said that to me when I had the flu last week I would have gone away sad because if I am always "fine and dandy" I have no good explanation for the days when I feel rotten. Better by far to be told that I am actually rotten and that something can be done about it. If I only think I'm sick, why are there some days I wish I were dead? If nothing is wrong, why do I cry some days?

No, it is much better to have Jesus come to my town on cold-filled autumn days and say:

You are sick, but I can cure you!
You are rotten, but I love you!
You are a damned fool, but I will save you!

Much better than have me die from sickness and sin and go to hell, leaving nothing behind but a gravestone inscribed:

I *told* you I was sick!

Jesus, my nose is running, my stomach is upset, I am all alone and tempted to act like a fool. Where is the end of the line for cures? I would like to have my turn.

Days of Sour Grapes

In the autumn of life there seem to be many more things that make me mad. Perhaps it's because I am more convinced that I have the answers to things and now nobody pays any attention. Nobody pays any attention to me – one who has been educated and bruised in the hard school of life! (Also in the autumn of life one has a tendency to romanticize how tough the past has been.)

In any case, one of the gospel stories that really "frosts" me is the story of those who come at the eleventh hour, work a little, and get full pay! I can just see them now, those "Johnny-come-lately crowds" who suddenly find religion at the end of their days and push their way in front of me to claim the reward that I have worked a lifetime for! (In the autumn of life one also has a tendency to romanticize how fervently one has worked for any ideal.)

On such days of envy I feel like sitting down with Jesus and complaining:

Lord, I read today the story of the Master who goes out at the eleventh hour and brings in those bums who spent the whole day standing idle, probably on the corner playing cards and drinking and looking at pretty girls and generally having just a fine time. And this Master paid them the same as he paid those who had worked all day. Those full-time workers must have been mad! There they were, tired and sweaty and dirty from a full day's work, just hanging on for that last hour so that they could get their pay and go home and collapse. It must have been tough on them to look up from their long back-breaking hoeing to see those new "*Ho-Ho-Hoing*" recruits, those "Johnny-come-lately converts" to the hard life, come swinging into the vineyard with their smart ideas and manicured hands. It must really have "frosted" those poor "slugs" who had worked all day!

What did you give them, Lord, those who worked all day? Oh, it was just fine and dandy for you to be kind to those who showed up late, the last hour, and lasted till the end. But what more did you do for those who lasted from the beginning? What did you do to those who were there from the beginning but who stopped work five minutes early? What did you do to those who had worked through the heat of the day but towards the end got sick or confused or just wandered away a bit too early? Did they get severance pay or sick leave or early retirement? What did you do about those who left early because they were bruised and embittered because your vineyard did not seem to be the same in the afternoon as when they started work in the morning? How about those who may have been driven mad by the heat of the midday sun? What did you do for them? What did you do about those who were too weak to work from early morning but did not realize it?

Were those who lasted till the end more sympathetic towards the late-comers than the early-leavers? Sometimes those who persevere can be cruel to old friends who fall by the wayside. They say things like "We knew he couldn't last! He was fooling around from the beginning!" Or they say, "If he had prayed more, things would have worked out!" But how does one pray, Lord, when insane from midday pressure or dulled by expectations come to nothing?

I know that everyone who spends any time in the vineyard with you, Lord, has a reward: namely, being with you for some time. But there is still the question that comes sometimes in the late afternoons of my autumn days: "What shall happen to me if I can't make it till the end?" It brings no answer, only terror.

Jesus, I am pleased that you are so kind to those who show up at the eleventh hour, but will you be as generous to those who try to work all day and yet fall apart five minutes before closing time? Will you be kind to them? Please tell me because I am afraid. My day is not yet finished and who knows whether I shall last?

Days of Clay

For some of us in our later years there are days when we seem to be responsible for all the evil in the world, or at least all the distress that surrounds us. We feel guilty about the distress of a loved one that we can't do much about. We feel distressed by the suffering we have caused and now can't remedy. On some days I seem to be overcome by a personal foolishness that only I perceive, a "not-living-up-to-promises" that only I perceive as broken. On such days I feel indeed like an old pot somewhat cracked by the fires of life, somewhat tarnished by the violent flames burning within me.

On such days it is easy for me to believe Paul's reminder that I am just clay, an old clay pot (2 Cor 4:7-16). It is hard on such days to believe that anything precious is contained in this crude vessel that is me. I am filled with autumn guilt for faults only dimly known. It is a terrible burden, this amorphous guilt, this feeling "no account," and it paralyzes me from doing the great works still open to me.

The solution, I know (but I cannot always believe because I am clay), is to realize that being clay there will always be some things I want to do and cannot do. Who ever heard of an infinite pot? And there will be some things that I can and should do but won't do, and consequently I will sometimes need forgiveness. But who ever heard of a pot that never needs washing? I need to accept the fact that I am a clay pot, to accept the fact of my limits and the need for absolution. I can't solve all the problems of those around me. And those I cause can be forgiven.

There is no use worrying about how good or bad I am. If potty I have any beauty, any heavenly quality at all, it is caused by Jesus the artist. I bring to the pot-making only a special rare mud, and even this has been loved into life by the Lord. I do not make myself anymore than a glistening vase forms its own shape on the potter's wheel.

Who is responsible for the suffering that sometimes spins off my life? Sometimes I am, to be sure, because I am a strange pot. I am free. I am a vessel of clay with imagination who is able to pretend to be more than he can be and to act as though less than he is. But sometimes I am the cause of the evil around me just because I am a foolish old pot that can dream and believe the silly (but somehow attractive) pretension that wishing will make it come true. Some evil is just the result of my clayness. As I whirl through life on Jesus' potter's wheel I spatter other lives with the all too human cry, "Here's mud in your eye!" Some evil is the result of my freedom and some comes from my foolishness and some just comes from my being clay. In any case there is no use spending my days moping about it.

It is much better to ask forgiveness and move on to tomorrow with the hope that things will be better. Who knows? Perhaps tomorrow someone will say "I love you" and mean it. Perhaps my new-found love will hold me and put me in a safe place and make me feel wanted and pretty. Maybe Jesus will pick me up as a bargain. Stranger pots are bought at flea markets. I do have slight cracks in my body and my lips are chipped. Jesus was a carpenter and should not mind getting his hands dusty. He won't be turned off by my being a little dirty. Perhaps he could use this old pot to keep his nails in.

Better in me than in his hands.

> Jesus, you made me and you could not make me other than to be clay. But you can fill me with your life and that life is bright enough to shine through even the dirt and blemishes of a lifetime. Don't let me cover your life with my bag of guilt on those days when I feel truly like an old clay pot.

Putting It All Together

Autumn days are fine days for writing history, especially my own. One day I sit down and suddenly realize that my past is quite expansive and that indeed my own personal past is much more interesting (to me at least) than any other historical study. There is the unreasoned conviction that if I could just spend a little time with myself I would be able to take my life and put it all together once and for all. Thus it is that I write for myself (and for Jesus) the story of my life.

Looking back I see my life as a continuous thread leading from darkness through light to darkness. (And then? . . . . But that hope for light beyond the second darkness must wait for another time.) I began in darkness, that damp-womb darkness of the first woman I was to love, hearing the throbbing life of a mother's body surrounding me, aware of her life before I was aware of my own. (Perhaps it is always thus: we find ourselves only through the love for another.)

Finally pulled into light upside-down and naked, like Peter on his final cross, I began the immense task of self-discovery. First it was my foot, ("Hello, Mr. Foot, are you me?"), and then my friend my thumb, happily embracing it with toothless gums, my first wet kiss of self-adulation. Day followed day and I sucked my thumb and played with my foot and thought, "Life is not half bad at all!" But it did not last. Enemies put shoes on my feet, pulled my thumb from my mouth and with horrified cries of "How dare you be happy!" sent me off to school.

They said that I had to go to school to learn the facts of life. To be honest, it was not too bad in the beginning. It was mostly play and song and I was happy. I painted pictures of realities only I could see: purple cows with orange legs, stick men and stick women with little to distinguish between them (the fantastic revelation of that difference came much later). My happy fantasies were ended when I realized that I was expected to know something, poor little me who did not even know himself very well was expected to know something about the universe! I was frightened. They had taken my thumb from my mouth and put shoes on my feet and told me to walk but never told me the direction. But I pulled myself together and bravely went about what all students learn to do. I faked it.

I piled degree upon degree so that I could get a fine job and pile dollar upon dollar and get a nice mansion on some Miami beach where all the mail comes addressed to OCCUPANT, a fitting title for one who with all his titles still does not know clearly what it is all about. Indeed, with all that education I learned little of importance about myself until the day I found that I was in love. Until I took that first mad leap into human love, until I took that first hesitant step towards Divine Love, there was little in life that had much meaning.

Lucky are we who in our lifetime find even one human being who truly loves us, who can care for us even when we don't care for ourselves. Through such human love we can begin to believe in the love that is Jesus-God. I begin to suspect who I am and where I am going when I see myself reflected in the eyes of one who loves me. And somewhere in my life I have had that wondrous experience. I have felt love and have seen the Lord.

I started knowing myself (apart from love) through my foot and thumb, and my scientific knowledge may never progress much beyond that. Indeed, I could even lose that modest awareness someday, completing my life cycle as a wrinkled baby on a bed of fading mind, perhaps unaware that the bulge in the bedclothes is my old friend my foot, perhaps mistaking it for a friendly visitor and happily chattering away to it about the wonderful things I had seen that day: purple cows with orange legs, stick men and stick women dancing merrily through the dust-flecked sunrays of my room.

Even that gentle end will not be a loss if somehow in my reverie I am able to know that I am still held in love by some dear friend, that even then I am loved by the burning love of Jesus-God.

My life then will have been all put together.

> Jesus, the older I get the more I realize that I am not that much different from the baby born so long ago. Perhaps that's why you sometimes allow us to end as we began, dreaming our way into new life. It really doesn't make too much difference who we are or what we know. The only important thing is that we be held by someone who loves us. Is that what you have been trying to teach me all these years? Hold me and tell me the answer.

Days of Trying to Forget

The trouble with autumn is that you have so many things to look back on that the number of real or imagined hurts can become magnified beyond any good sense. In my autumn days I find it hard sometimes to forgive. I find it almost impossible to forget. It seems as though I am made of soft wax. I am easily cut open and once wounded the hurt hardens and becomes a permanent blemish on the smooth surface of my life, a jagged chasm reaching deep inside me and touching nerves forever hidden to others. I cannot forget my hidden hurts.

Oh, over the years I may build a thin cosmetic covering over my wound so that people will not notice. The construction may be so skillful that others come to envy the apparent calmness of my life. But deep down inside the wound is still open and it throbs. I cannot even stand being in the presence of the one who caused the hurt, so shattering is the memory to me. Nothing I or any other human can do will take away the pain. Only Jesus can rub it away.

When I lose a loved one, only Jesus can fill the gap. When I injure those I love, only Jesus can take away the agony of guilt. When I have been made a fool of, when I have been made to feel worthless, when I have been made to feel unloved and unlovable, only Jesus-God can take away the hurt. And he can do it only eventually. Even he may not be able to make the hurt less here and now.

He knows that. That's why he insists only that we forgive (Matt 18:21). He doesn't demand that we forget. He knows that we can't, not right away. He knows because although he forgave those who beat him and those who crowned him and those who stripped him and those who nailed him, he did not forget what the pain was like until his final death sigh of relief. We forget some hurts only when we die.

Jesus is saying to me much more than "Forgive!" He is saying:

> Don't wound others! Love others so deeply and constantly that they will have no wounds to try to forget. How many times should you forgive? Seventy times seven! How many times may you wound? Not even once! I allowed you to kill me so that I might forgive you. Do not now kill each other because I cannot save you from the pain of wounds you can't forget.

That's what Jesus-God says. I hope I don't forget.

> Jesus, help me mask over the pains accumulated in my lifetime. But let me realize that they are there so that I will hesitate to reach out to strike down those I love. The injury I cause those who need my love is an injury hard to forget, by them and by me.

Days for Making Decisions (Changing My Mind)

Over years of life I have developed a wonderful capacity to make decisions. Why, I can make a thousand decisions a day. For example:

"I shall type this page."
"No, I shall do some reading, instead."
"But then there is always that other alternative!"

Indeed on some days I change my mind so frequently that I have little time for anything else. Like Buridan's jackass in the story, I stand immobilized among the equally unimportant alternatives of my usual days.

The ease with which I make decisions (change my mind) tempts me to believe that I could even now change my whole life if I would just put my mind to it. I am tempted to believe that if I really tried I could make that grand converting choice that would uproot my settled ways and set me on some new and seemingly more fruitful track. If Paul could change so easily (I say to myself) from persecutor to preacher of Christ, why can't I? Why can't I say, "No! Despite how I have been, henceforth I shall be thus and so (or maybe something else)." Of course it is easier said than done. Even if I could make up my mind about what I finally wanted to be, it is hard to change. The longer I live, the more encumbered do I become by habits and loves not easily dismissed.

We sing pretty songs about changing our lives for the sake of new loves but reality always whispers, "Lot's of luck, fella!" Certainly it is possible for new loves to conquer old warriors but it is no easy trick. Not only is it difficult to teach old dogs new tricks, on some days you can't even get their attention.

And thus it is that although it may seem easy for someone to divorce his wife or for me suddenly to adopt a new life, it is not done without pain. I carry a lot of history with me. And despite all my courageous decisions (changing my mind) I am the same old pot after as before. The day after I took my religious vows I still had to shave. I was as ugly as before. I had pains in all the accustomed places. These old familiar things in my life make it terribly difficult to change my life radically overnight.

Thus, I had better decide today to begin to love Jesus completely. I can't depend on making such a decision at the last moment. "But, on the other hand . . ."

Jesus, in my autumn days don't let me dream too much about other lives in other places. I am too encumbered by life to change much now. But the dream of radical change can prevent me from being really good at what I am and could lessen your love for me. Because you love only what I am, not what I might have been.

Days of Hurting

I remember someone saying once, "What I just did must be terribly right because it certainly does hurt."

Why is it that doing the right things sometimes causes so much pain? I suppose it is not so much that what we finally had the guts to do was right as it is that we got ourselves into such a mess trying to avoid doing it that it had to hurt when the boom was finally lowered. It's like avoiding going to the dentist when we should. It hurts all the more when we finally do go.

The pain is especially intense when the one we hurt is a loved one – a child or a parent or a very dear friend – and we realize that we could have prevented the hurt if only we had acted more sensibly sometime before. If we had not pretended all along that things were just fine, it would not be so hard to state now that things really had been bad. But of course, in our great "wisdom," we had kept our mouths shut. The stupidity occurred, and now the only way out is painful.

We hurt and those we love are hurting too, but now we must stand firm in the midst of our shared tears, convinced that finally the right thing has been done. We are convinced because we feel so rotten.

Maybe that's what Jesus meant when he said I must take up my cross. It means not only that I must bear my own cross but also that sometimes I must watch loved ones bear crosses fashioned by my stupidity. Is that why he began his death-week riding on a donkey? Did he want to warn me that most of the suffering in life begins with a well-intentioned jackass?

Jesus, give me the strength to be firm. And let the hurt in my loved one's heart quickly pass.

Days of Leaving

Two friends left the ministry the other day. Bill died and Joe will marry. In both cases it was an affair of the heart.

Like me, they were no longer "chickens." They had grown old and weathered in the work. But then changes in life are not unusual in the early autumn of life. The temptation to change is very common. We are not so anxious for change in the spring. We are more concerned to taste the fullness of the moment. There will always be more time (we say) for other things. Springtime is the season of hope. We taste fruit not fully ripe and say, "Things will get better. I will wait." But as spring goes to summer and summer to fall and nothing happens, a seed of doubt is planted: "Has the trail been lost? Am *I* lost?"

If we become ill (as Bill was) and feel darkness rushing to meet us, we may not try new things. Rather, we stay with the usual, as unsatisfactory as it may be, and wait quietly for that last great happening, our death. If doubts come and we still feel the vigor of late summer, we may be prepared to change our lives even though we are facing the autumn of our days. Autumn is seen then as a time for new loves and new tasks. We snatch any new brilliance quickly. We are harried by our hurry. We rush to new possibilities thinking that there will be little time for new adventures.

Perhaps the impatience of early autumn presages our impatience to drive forward through death into eternity. One thing is certain: we need a loving hand to hold when the chill doubts of autumn sweep across our lives.

Jesus, take care of Bill and Joe. And take care of me in the autumn of my life. Don't let me be so distracted by new songs that I no longer hear the constancy of your melody playing within me.

Dusty Angels

There are two familiar descriptions that sum up the paradox of being human. On the one hand we are told that we are a little less than the angels; on the other, we are reminded that we came from dust and to dust we shall return. How odd! We are then dusty angels, soaring birds with waxed-on wings. No wonder we are mixed up! We are always tempted to live beyond ourselves, and the danger terrifies us.

Each day we are called to go beyond ourselves, to dare new things, think new thoughts, try new loves. We dream of being gods and we know we must try to be godly. To be humans we must try to be with the gods. At the same time we are reminded every morning as we peer at the moldy reflection in our mirror that dust is our reality also. In shock we realize that we are creatures, that no matter what we do or how far we go we shall never be in complete control of things. We are reminded that no matter how successful we are our reluctant body will certainly fail, and probably in a most embarrassing way. Paul had his sting of the flesh and Augustine had migraine. Why should we be different?

Of course there are some moments when it almost seems that we are gods, but the moments never last very long. Nature calls at unpropitious moments. We get hungry or we just fall asleep. We can imitate gods only in those brief seconds between the call of creature-needs. We can only preen our angel wings when our dust settles.

Our constant problem is how best to react to this tension. Some play it safe. They build narrow existences within which they play with self-made toys and fictions, fictions such as "It is better to be safe than sorry" or "It is better never to dare" or "It is better not to have loved than to have loved and lost." Sad lives are these safe lives. They lead to a life of closed windows and shuttered doors, an existence unhealthy for house or human.

But there is another alternative. We can face the fact of our being creatures. We can face the fact that we are in need of outside support and begin the task of looking for someone to hold onto. If there is no one there, it may make sense to try for the "safe" life. Better a small raft to hang onto than an unending swim in the darkness. But we should try to see if there is anyone out there first.

Christians are told that the sea is not empty. We are told that there is someone beyond our little lives, beyond our certain deaths. There is someone who will support our creatureliness and help us get beyond ourselves. We are told that the same Christ who called us into this mixed-up human life will support us through death. And then we shall truly see how through our adventures in the dust we have won the life of God in us.

I think I will get my wings ready.

> Jesus, don't let me close up all my doors and windows in trying to be safe. If I am so closed up, how can you get in? And if you can't be with me, this dusty old house might just be condemned.

Days for Wondering About the End

In the days of autumn I sometimes feel like the disciples felt when they went to Jesus wondering what it would be like in the end. I would like to know (but only on some days) how it will end for me. Jesus answered the disciples' question by talking about the sky darkening, stars falling, a shaking of heaven and earth, a coming of the Son of Man with trumpets blaring and angels spread out before him calling together all the elect (Matt 13:24-32). The disciples were delighted! They naturally assumed that Jesus was speaking about the end of their lives and that they would be among the elect. Although their passage into heaven was something of a holocaust, it was impressive and made them feel important. Perhaps they felt like bit-players in a Hollywood disaster movie, the street-cleaner in *Earthquake* or the doorman of the *Towering Inferno*. Of course they missed the point completely. Jesus was not telling them how they would end their days but how all days would end. Their ending was quite different. Much quieter though no less final.

So too, it may be the case that I shall depart not with a shout but with a whisper. Perhaps I shall be like the "Suitcase Man," whose story was reported in November 1976. Perhaps Jesus will come to me as he must have come to the "Suitcase Man".

> Jesus was in Detroit for a few days to visit friends. He had arrived by bus. Even God does not drive in Detroit if he can

avoid it. And thus it was that he came upon the "Suitcase Man". The man stood in the bus station with a cheap suitcase beside him. He told people that it contained all that he owned. He lived in the station for fifty-two days before the police finally took him away. He told those who asked: "I must stay here until I have worked things out. There is no place to go." Some said that he had a wife and child someplace. When asked about them he said, "We had a good life . . . but I've lost a lot. And right now I must stay here until I've worked it out." He was thirty years old.

Jesus waited there until the police took him away. He went with him to the hospital and stayed with him till the end. As far as anyone could tell, the poor man never did "work things out" but good people took care of his physical needs and Jesus would talk quietly with him and there was a kind of peace around him.

Eventually he died and Jesus buried him. As he was leaving the cemetery with a few friends they asked him, "How shall it be at the end for us, Lord?" And Jesus said: "It may be warm and joyful. It may be exciting and fearful. Or it may be quietly absurd, as it was for this little man. But I will be with all of you in your final days. And after the end you will be with me and the 'Suitcase Man' and we shall all be happy together and at peace."

Thank you, Jesus.

4   Final Days

What will be the color of my final days? It should be something restful. Evenings are dark with good reason. The human animal can best rest when it is dark, and prepare for the next busy day. It is difficult to sleep in the shadowless glare of a noon sun. I have done it, but only on occasions of exhausted collapse. Evening sleep is more natural. My dark-gentled night rest is as much a part of my living as the frenetic activity of my day.

The color of those final days before my sleep should indeed be dark. But it should not be black. In an absolute darkness there is no richness, no presence. Absolute black is fearsome. In such black it seems that nothingness is ready to devour me. And that emptiness is not the character of my final days. My hours are not a void. In my final days it is rather as though I were being gently wrapped in rich purple robes, snuggling down in their embrace to await the coming of some new dawn. The purple that surrounds me is peaceful. I have put aside my toys, closed my books, and now wait sleepily as my world slowly darkens. The deep purples and blues of the deepening dusk seem to encourage the twinkling stars to rush past me to meet the glorious sun of the coming day.

There is no fear, no anxiety, as I slip off to sleep. I remember the story of all my days with their joys and loves and am satisfied. I close my eyes easily in the purpled darkness and wait without fear for him who is to come. I wait for that great good friend who has come so often before and is now preparing to take me to my fine new day.

Fear of Dying

It is best to begin by admitting the fact: I am afraid of dying. The fear persists despite all the years of praying and hoping and believing. Despite all the preaching about resurrection, despite all the learned lectures about death and life, despite the gentle words of assurance said so confidently at numberless wakes and funerals, the fear of my death persists. Like Jesus I cry to the Father, "If you will, take this cup away from me" (Luke 22:42). But I know it will not pass. "[Jesus] prayed even more fervently; his sweat was like drops of blood, falling to the ground" (Luke 22:44). Yes, I am afraid of dying.

It is not that my consoling phrases or confident teachings or brave preachings were hypocritical. They were as honest as my present fear. I meant what I said about resurrection. I believed in it and do now believe in it. But when I spoke I was always speaking about the death and resurrection of Jesus or the death and resurrection of each and every human being. I never spoke about the death of Donald. Perhaps I cannot. I cannot talk about my death. I can only go through it.

My dying is something like my going to the dentist for the first time. Even though I know I must do it, even though I know it is for my own good, even though someone I love has told me that it will work out just fine, the fear remains because I can't see how it will be to go through the event and I don't know how I shall be when it is all over. And death is worse than going to the dentist. There are fewer survivors that I can actually see and talk to. I can't get the feeling of how it will be on the other side of death-decay as I can for the land on the other side of tooth-decay.

For all these reasons I have now in my later years a conscious fear of dying. Oh, I suspect that it was present too at earlier times but then it was more easily covered over. I still remember the Ash Wednesdays of my youth when the ashes on my forehead were more a sign of my Catholicity than a reminder of my contingency. They were a sheltering sign to "Sister" that I had gone to church at the proper time and done the appropriate thing. They were thus a protection from injury rather than a projection of death. How could "Child-Donald" worry about returning to dust when he had the conviction based on past experience that the ashes of that first Lenten Wednesday were necessary steps on the way to the delights of Easter candy and the frolic of another fine earthly spring.

Ash Wednesday did not move me until much later when I placed ashes on the brow of a dying loved one. Looking into her eyes I saw the reflection of her death and mine. And my heart was crushed by sorrow and fear.

Now in my autumn days I can remember many dear friends and family who have died. I am forced to face the fact that my own death is out there someplace in the future, rushing to meet me. The event will be unique because though death is common, this death will be mine. There is no guidebook. There is no precedent. "It is appointed for man (Donald) once to die, and after that the judgment" (Heb 9:27).

What can I do? Perhaps only this: admit the fear and go on with what I know, this day of life and whatever days are left to me. During these days I can speak with love to others about life and death, and in our gentle conversations perhaps Jesus will speak to us and calm some of our fright.

Jesus, in my days of waiting for death let me know
that I am not alone. Let me know that you and others
care for me as I wait for that last great experience of
this life, my death.

The Black Spot

In quiet moments I get this odd feeling that I am slipping away. It is hard to put into words. The feeling comes and goes. The other night it came suddenly as I drove a dark road alone. There was this blackness inside me, like a growth. It seemed very tiny, almost invisible, but it was alive. Over time there was a movement, now a swelling, now a collapsing. As I sit here it definitely seems alive and I am afraid. I am compelled to believe that no matter how tiny it is now, it will grow and grow and finally consume me. It is a living, growing gap in me. It is the beginning of my death.

Most of us, if we are lucky, start life full. We are filled with life and curiosity and hope. When we are young we are brim-filled with vitality. So it seems now, looking back. But then after a while a little gap in the fullness appears. There is a hole in the seamless fabric of our lives. There is a breach in life. There is a touch of insecurity and it cries: "Today you live, it is true. But you cannot mend *this* hole in your life." We realize then that we are pregnant with the seed of our destruction.

We bear our strange visitor as an unwilling parent with no hope of relief. No, it will never leave us. Our dark growth is bound to us by a cord of steel. Like some parasite it is always inside us, eating, eating, eating away, until it is everything and we are nothing.

Some are overpowered by the thought of such a presence. They become fascinated by the darkness in their lives. They direct all their attention to it. They become isolated from all else. To be sure, they are alive, but they are alone with their darkness. They are insane.

Others, like Lady Macbeth, cry, "Out, Damned Spot!" and when it does not disappear they try to forget it. They try to forget that strange lightless growth, that vacuum, that emptiness in them. Of course it still continues to grow despite their ignoring it.

At its worst the awareness of this dark breach in our lives makes all else seem worthless. Our entire life seems nothing more than a purposeless passing of time. *Nothing* is happening. *Nothing* is growing. Our life seems a process whereby we become *nothing*.

Most of us try to cope with the feeling in some way. Some cope through love. We hold someone dear to ourselves and it helps. We clutch our love and feel the beating heart of another life. We hold each other tighter and tighter, desperately trying to make one out of two. There is a momentary ecstasy. Perhaps it comes because for an instant we dream that our union has created a greater something that can withstand even death, that growing nothingness in each of us. There is a momentary peace. Perhaps it is because in the amazement that someone could care about us in our weakness and fear, our emptiness does not seem empty. We forget the emptiness inside us. We forget, that is, until we are alone or driving down a dark highway separated from our love.

That is the worst time of all, when we are separated from our love. When we have loved and the love suddenly is taken from us, the gap in our lives seems like a huge vacuum into which our lives rush. The black nothingness inside us increases like a mountain stream, by leaps and bounds. It is suddenly multiplied by its easy victory over the space left by absent love. The victory calls for no great celebration. There is no fanfare, just a quiet occupation of the crumbling castle that is us, long since deserted by our love.

It is a terrible thing for one with this Black Spot to lose love. It is for this reason that we become so terrified when our loved one becomes sick. For then it seems as though the terrible growth, that Black Spot, that growing gap in our lives, has spread its infection to our dear one. We cry out in fear and try to suck the dying of our beloved into ourselves. For a brief moment love conquers our thirst for life. We try to trade our remaining fullness for the emptiness we see growing in the fading life of the one who has captured our heart. But deep down we know that we cannot trade our life for another's death. Our coping fails when our loved one is lost. We are weakened by past joy and present emptiness. It seems suddenly great good sense to submit, to embrace our nothingness as we once embraced our beloved, with our own hands.

Thinking about such things as I drove down the dark highway, I sensed that the slight opening in the fullness of my life had exploded into some awesome black hole, a huge galactic maw where there was no space or time, dark because so terribly consuming that even light could not escape. Irresistibly it draws all to itself, and me especially. As I drive through life I seem to be falling into it. What I was, what I am, what I hope to be: all these things are falling irrevocably through that huge dark opening in my life to become finally just nothing. Or so it seems.

Faith tells me that this is not the end. The story of resurrection tells me that the gap in my life is not death. It is God's life growing in me. It is God's life that eats at me, consuming my fragile existence so that its space can be filled with the life of God. It is indeed a strange, wonderful message. I rush towards death but I should do so joyfully because I know that waiting for me there will be the living God. It is the same God who even now lives in me, in those growing dark gaps in my life which so frighten me sometimes.

Jesus, don't let me be too afraid as I move towards
death. Let me understand that the less there is of me

the more room there is for you. Let me embrace my dear ones without fear. Even though we may be separated for a while, we shall be reunited forever one day through your life, in your arms.

The Passing of Old Friends

There will come a day, if I live to be very old, when I shall suddenly realize that most of those I have known and treasured are gone. My friends have gone and left me. It is then that I will cease to fear my own passage and begin to long for that place where all my friends are. On the day of the passing of old friends I will feel as though my time has also passed. My bus has left without me. I will feel like the kid standing on the corner watching the bus to summer camp disappear down the road, hearing the shouts and laughter grow fainter and fainter until I am left alone in silence.

This feeling that occurs in later days is quite different from the feeling experienced during my springtime days when a friend dies. In those green times I was surprised and frightened when a friend passed on. It seemed out of place that anyone young should die, that anyone my age should die. It was almost as though I expected some solemn promise that none of the friends of my youth should ever be taken from me.

It is quite different when we are in our final days. When we are older and weaker there is a different kind of surprise. We are surprised that anyone our age is alive, especially ourselves. We are not surprised when old friends die. We wonder that we have survived. We may even feel cheated that we are still going on. It is easy to wish for death when those we love have gone before us and there seems to be nothing of importance left for us to do.

When a beloved wife or husband dies it is even worse. Taken from us is that one with whom we have shared our most intimate thoughts, that one we have touched in love and been foolish with and held quietly in the soft darkness of evening, that one with whom we have danced and sung on life's golden beaches. When our dearest dies we die too, although we may walk the earth for a few more years. When our dear friends die, when our beloved dies, then we need to have Jesus-God walk with us. As the shadows darken our life we fear death less than we fear being alone, separated from those with whom we have shared our lives.

We have missed the bus. We wait anxiously for our time to leave. We want to get moving so that we can catch up with our heart, which has been taken away piece by piece by our departed loves.

> Jesus, if at all possible don't let me be left alone at the end. Leave a friend or two, some beloved, with whom I can share my last days. At least let me feel your presence. Then I can wait for reunion with the others more patiently.

The Meaning of Success

In one's final days it is natural to look back and wonder if life was worth the trouble. It depends on what success truly is. Who knows? It may just be that in the limited lifetime that is mine success is nothing more than finding the Lord. When does this happen? It is hard to predict. There is no one way for meeting the Lord.

There was this man, for example, who was ordained after years and years of preparation. He celebrated his one and only Mass and then went crazy, or so we say. He continued to live, but withdrawn completely inside himself, hiding there deep inside, still with us and yet absent. It saddened and scared us to see him leave that way and so we "put him away" because we thought him out of contact with reality (our reality). He could no longer live a fruitful productive life, or so we say.

But who knows? Perhaps he found the Lord in his one and only celebration and became so excited by the discovery that he rushed away in his joy, leaving behind his still living body for us to tend.

We feel so sad for him. But should we? If in fact he found the Lord, why should we weep? Oh, we should feel sorry, but for ourselves because he cannot tell us when we face our final days what success truly means.

He still lives with us happily even though his mind and spirit have been swept away to that place still unknown to me in these my final days. He smiles because he is in the joyous place where he and the Lord walk hand in hand through endless day.

> Jesus, help me not be sad looking back. There is still time to find you and be a success. Come now, so I can have one final party.

A Day for Masking: A Day for Unmasking

In the Druid calendar November 1 was the beginning of a new year. It was a feast of thanksgiving to the Sun-God for all the rich harvest of the previous year. The evening before the feast was a time when the film between this life and the next was very thin. It was a time for talking to the dead. It was a time for talking to loved ones about the life that had passed and the life that was to come.

For us Halloween has become a feast of the young. It is a time of hope, of fantasy, of amazing worlds in which anything is possible. The young understand the feast best of all because they understand what it means to be on the edge of a new life filled with mystery. They come to our doors laughing in their fine costumes. They dress as tiny ballerinas or supermen or ladybugs or pigs or frogs or pumpkins or ghosts or goblins, fantasy creatures never seen in the dull reality of adult life. On Halloween the children remind us that we live in a world of infinite possibility. They remind us that we live on the edge of a new life where infinity is real. It is nice that we give treats to the tiny fantasies at our Halloween doors. We remind ourselves that the eve of new life need not be sad even though it marks the end of life that has gone before.

Halloween is a night for masking. But the masks are innocent and cheery. We do not hide behind them. We are showing off. And our friends know the persons behind the strange disguises. On Halloween we dance and laugh together at the glorious silliness of our pretense.

All Hallows Day is a Christian feast celebrating our final unmasking. We anticipate the day when Jesus-God will lead us through death and take from our faces the masks we have used in this life. For the first time we shall see our true selves reflected in the eyes of Jesus-God. Sometimes I am fearful when I think of that day. Perhaps it is because of a recurring dream, a terrible dream that returned again and again in my early years.

I dreamed that on the night before my own personal All Hallows I was awakened by a knock on my door. I opened the door to discover a tall figure standing on the threshold. He was dressed in fine, rich robes and on his face there was a glittering silver mask.

"Who are you?" I asked.

"I am you," the figure responded, "and tomorrow I must go to meet my God."

I invited the apparition in, but insisted, "First you must take off your mask so that I can see my true face."

He slowly lifted the mask and I screamed in horror. It was not that the face revealed was so terribly deformed. There was no face at all.

Later on when I grew older I came to understand the meaning of the dream. It was warning me that if I spend my whole life pretending to be something other than I am, the reality that is me will melt away. That little thing that had been me, that tiny unimportant thing, that "me-thing" that shamed me so much, that "me-thing" that God had loved and brought into being, that "me-thing" that God had died to save, that "me-thing" had died of my pretense and now there was nothing for Jesus-God to see. I understood then that hell was having Jesus-God look for me and having him find nothing.

As I grew in an awareness of Jesus' love for every human "me-thing," another dream grew in my life. As before there was the mysterious stranger at my door on All Hallows eve.

"Who are you?" I asked again.

"I am you and now I must go and stand before my God."

As before, I invited the apparition to rest but insisted that first he remove his glittering silver mask so that I could see myself as I really was. He took off the mask and I cried with joy. I saw the face of Jesus.

Indeed I laughed with joy because I realized that when the time comes to see my face reflected in the eyes of my God I will see not my old face but his. I understood that he did much more than simply love me and create me and die for me. Jesus-God had taken that simple unimportant stuff that was me and had made it into himself. He had flooded me with his life!

In my dream I sang the great Christian hymn of triumph: *"I live, no longer I, but Christ lives in me!"* (Gal 2:20)

> Jesus, don't let me so hide myself in masks in this life that you can't find me in the next. Take my clay and mold from it your face. Then I shall see beauty reflected when my time comes to see myself in your eyes.

The Christmas of My Winter

There will come a day when I shall celebrate my last Christmas. This I know for sure. How shall I feel on such a day? What does Christmas mean for those at the end of life?

It is a feast for the very old as much as for the very young. Indeed, the fact that God became man may become a central fact for me at the end of life. When I was young I could get along quite well without God at Christmas, or so it seemed. It was easy to tinsel and decorate my life with distractions, fill it with friends and folly. I had plenty of time. I was fully and irrevocably alive, or so it seemed.

When I am coming to my end and am conscious of the fact, the Christmas message of Christ's presence in my tattered world may be my greatest consolation. As I pass into the next world my communication with this one may dim. I will not be able, perhaps, to speak easily to my friends nor they to me. They will talk of life and I will talk of death. Only God can truly understand me then. Humans may speak to me in life. Only God can speak to me in death.

It is important for me now, in the vigor of my life, to make Jesus live in each today. Then he will be born again on the day of my death and I will recognize him. I must begin now to prepare for that last Christmas because life is passing. Plato described human life as a cavern in which each of us is trapped for a short time. The "drip, drip, drip" I sometimes hear in my quiet times is the splashing of my jeweled "nows" into the shadowed pool of my past. My life is strong now but it is passing.

It is the flash of a firefly in the night. It is the breath of buffalo in the winter time. It is the little shadow which runs across the grass and loses itself in the sunset.*

Life is passing and I must prepare for the final birth of Jesus in my life. Christ will be present to me at the end but I could be like some residents of Bethlehem and not recognize him. What a terrible tragedy that would be if on that holy night of my last Christmas I did not recognize the one who comes to visit. What a terrible mistake it would be to close the door on the stranger standing with me on the threshold of my death, saying, "I am sorry, Sir. I have no time for you now. Just now I must die . . . alone."

> Jesus, let me get accustomed to you every day of my life so that I will recognize you on the day of my death. It is easy to forget the birthday of a stranger. One never forgets the birthday of a friend. Be a friend now so that I will not forget the last birthday you will spend with me in this life.

*From the sayings of the American Indian, Crowfoot, in *Touch the Earth: A Self Portrait of Indian Existence,* ed. T. C. McLuhan (New York: Pocket Books, Inc., Div. of Simon & Schuster, Inc., 1972) 12.

No Sorrow: No Regrets

The best life is one that ends with no regrets, with no great bitterness about the past. It is a blessing to spend final days without cursing what has gone before. Only on days of no regrets can one wait peacefully and with anticipation for what is to come next.

One great fear I have is that I might end as a bitter old man, mumbling to myself about past injuries and injustices, looking furiously at the world around me, complaining that no one has ever given me due and proper respect.

It is painful to see such bitterness at the end of life. It must be worse to experience it. Some seem to die with a scream of rage. They are tied into bitter knots about the past. They cannot conceive that any future without oblivion can be any better. They curse their fate.

They cry for justice. They must have revenge on those who have mistreated them, and until this "justice" is done, heaven can indeed wait. Heaven has little meaning for them, so dedicated are they to seeing the rest of the world firmly placed in hell.

Such bitterness is a possibility for any human. I see it is possible for me. The older I get the more sensitive to injury I become, perhaps because I perceive that I cannot protect myself, I cannot flee from my life and start over anew. It wasn't as difficult when I was young and mobile. Real or supposed affronts were easily forgotten. When my love was rejected or laughed at I could move on saying, "So much the worse for them! There are others who want my love!" When my ambitions were frustrated there still seemed to be an infinite number of better opportunities. It still seemed that I could be almost anything I wanted to be. Rejections of my talent seemed to me to be injuries to the one rejecting. "They will be sorry someday," I said, "when they see what my life has become and how they 'missed the boat' by ignoring me!"

Such youthful dreaming is impossible in the days of autumn. What I could be has become what I am and now I must justify my actual deficiency to that most severe critic of all: myself. This I do by arguing that indeed I have always had hidden talents and the reason, the *only* reason, they have been unproductive is that they have gone unappreciated by a cruel and selfish and malicious and stupid world. Self-righteousness becomes fury and the last days become fruitless times of railing against the injustices of a world that has rejected such a lovely fine person like me.

God, I fear ending like that! I hope the older I get the sillier I get. Good humor is the only protection against bitterness. To be able to laugh at the world and mostly at myself is the best way to keep a good stomach. To be constantly amazed that anyone seems to care for me, to feel honored that anyone has accepted my love, to be surprised that any of my castles are still standing, to be awed that I have been able to drive through life so far without killing anyone: these are the precious attitudes that will keep me gentle in my final days.

> Jesus, give me the great gift of the Spirit: silliness. Let me take my life lightly and end it as I began, playing peacefully on the beach with some dear friend. Let me smile in my later days remembering that you at least appreciate me and that in some bumbling way I

have been able to do just exactly what you wanted me to do. Everything else is so much straw.

"Lazarus, Get Up!"

The trouble with me (and the rest of the human race) is that I see reality from the narrow perspective of my own experience. I see life from this particular "here" in this particular "now." Consequently it is hard to be truly convinced that things could be much better in some foreign place at some different time. Thus when I was on the sunrise side of my life it was hard for me to imagine the beauty that awaited me when I finally clambered over the barren rocks at the peak and began my descent into the sunset. We are where we are and we just don't know, we truly don't know any better.

I thought of this fact as I was reading the story of Lazarus. When Lazarus died it was automatically assumed by his sisters and his friends that he was in a terribly unfortunate situation. It was assumed that if Lazarus were asked (and there is no indication that they even thought to get his views on the question) he would certainly choose to return to them in that barren graveyard warmed by a weak winter-sun. They asked Jesus to do something, but by *something* they meant to bring Lazarus back to them. Martha cried out, "If you had been here, Lord, my brother would not have died" (John 11:21).

Perhaps she and Mary and Lazarus had all been on the sunrise side of life. She remembered her brother as young and vigorous and ambitious, with a great future before him. The good that she wanted for him, the only good that she could understand, was that he be plucked from the grave and be returned to the fullness of the only life she knew. When Jesus stood before the grave of Lazarus for the first time there was only one sort of miracle that the people could accept. When Jesus commanded, "Untie him and let him go free!" the only acceptable result was to have Lazarus with all his usual blemishes and infirmities walk from the cave to rejoin his friends and family in the supposedly wonderful world of the rock-strewn graveyard warmed by that weak winter-sun. It was the only life and happiness that they knew.

Well, Jesus did as they wished. Lazarus came back to life. He lived for a while longer and then, of course, he died again. We don't know for sure how it went that second time around. I suspect that it was quite different. When Lazarus died the second time Jesus had *his* way. He did not give in to the narrow perspective on life taken by humans. The second time Lazarus died the story probably went something like this:

> Lazarus was an old man bothered much by arthritis and dimming sight and dimming hearing and dimming mind. He was in the winter of his life and the growing cold darkness prevented him from clutching the life he had. He was ready and waiting for any new spring. He spent much of his days and nights remembering good times past with friends and family. The memories kept him from feeling lonely, for in fact he was very much alone. Those who had wept at his first funeral were now gone themselves. His sisters and his friends were dead. Indeed, he shook his head in sadness sometimes, thinking about it. After all that fuss about bringing him back, his sisters had gone and left him! It was as if he had been pressured to return to a party only to find on his arrival that the rest of the crowd had run out the other door.
>
> The day finally came when his life gave out for the second time and he died. By this time there were few who knew him very well and thus strangers carried him to the graveyard. After an appropriate prayer they returned to their business. Jesus was looking on (as he always is) and felt compelled to play some part in this second burial. He felt the need to close off the story of Lazarus in some way. So he went to the graveyard and asked the attendant, "Where have you laid Lazarus?" The attendant replied, "Lazarus who?" but after a moment of searching his records he remembered and led Jesus and a few curious bystanders to a cave and pointed to a pile of grave-cloths in the corner. Jesus commanded, "Untie him and let him go free!" They took away the linen wrappings and fell back in surprise. There was nothing there.
>
> The story went about (as at the resurrection of Jesus) that the body had been stolen. The poor humans could not imagine any other explanation because their vision was limited by their narrow world that ended with the grave. But Jesus knew

the full story and he laughed. He knew where Lazarus was. He knew that for the first time and finally his good friend was free!

Jesus, in the twilight of my life don't let me be afraid to run through the sunset to that world of freedom where I shall dance with Mary and Martha and Lazarus and you.

Flowers on a Grave

In the midst of the university I found a cemetery, a most effective class for those who would listen.

The stones were tiny.
No great monuments were needed to mark lives
lived without fuss.
Someday I may rest there.

Against one of the stones rested a bouquet,
flowers alive but dying,
resting on one who died believing in life.

The blossoms spoke soundless words
remembering a dead one's life,
words that I have often said to my absent loves:
"I miss you. Someday we shall be together again."

The silent words of the dying flowers were somehow louder
than the noises of the young students
playing at the games of life.
They proclaimed, "Great love cannot be contained
by a grave!"

As those poor flowers dissolved,
trying to break through the earth
into the grave of the beloved,
so did my loving God break out of his tomb
to lead me with my dear, dear friends

from this land of dying flowers
to his land of life and everlasting love.

Jesus, did they put flowers on your grave? I imagine they were surprised when you got up the next
morning and gave the blossoms to your friends.

Days of Infancy

In these the later days of my life I have this increasing passion to
leave my wordprints in space and time. Through marks on paper such
as these I may touch the spirit of others. Then if the day comes when I
shall no longer be able to communicate, someone may come upon my
marks and say (to no one in particular), "Now that must have been a
fine fellow! Perhaps I could have loved him."

The passion becomes more frantic as I draw closer to final days.
Who knows? Perhaps at the end my thought will cease and I shall
finish my days in a second infancy. Perhaps I shall live through final
days with my mind all but dead, not knowing the present, much less
remembering the past, gazing vacantly at a beloved without recogni-
tion (how terrible to be in the presence of loveliness and not be
moved), losing interest in and control over my body's functions, spending final days as a diapered wizened baby with no prospect for growth.

Dedicated staff in nursing homes (and what a dedication that is)
have told me that those with failed minds are truly at peace. They do
not know what they have been. They do not realize what they are. This
may be the case at the very end. But I have looked into the eyes of a
dear one who was in process, who still had enough sense to know what
was happening to her. And I could see the fright in her eyes. Before the
glitter finally left her clear blue eyes, I could see her pain. She could
not tell me what she was going through as sense slipped away. Nor
could she tell me the reason for her smile, the source of the peace in
her empty gaze, when her mind altogether stopped paying attention to
this world. The senile are not interested in writing books like this for
us. They talk about their experiences only to friends from another
world – friends with whom they can feel comfortable.

Perhaps the oblivion that comes is not all that bad. The switching off of the mind may just be a gift given by Jesus-God to a select few, those few he chooses to spend their final days more intimately with him. Senility may be the ultimate form of contemplation. It could be that my beloved's eyes were vacant because she was looking somewhere else, into the eyes of Jesus-God. Perhaps she did not eat because she was already tasting a food from heaven. Perhaps the trembling in her limbs was a sign that she was already dancing with the Lord. When I held her hand I could feel the pressure of her fingers. She seemed to know I was there. Perhaps she was trying to draw me with her, to take my hand and place it in the hand of the Jesus-God who already held her. But she never told me what it was like. She was busy elsewhere.

Knowing so little of what it is like to spend final days without a mind, I fear it. And I make these marks and pass them on so that perchance when I am dead and gone, or alive still but gone in mind and interest, someone will see my marks and say (to no one in particular), "Now that must have been a fine fellow! Perhaps I could have loved him."

If someone loved me, I think I would know. Even if I had closed up my mind to this life, Jesus-God would pass on the word. I would be happy for a moment, remembering the fun of this life. And then I would go back to dancing madly with Jesus-God, who could not wait for my death to start my "Welcome Home!" party.

> Jesus, give me the light to see you when the lights of this world begin to fade for me. Make your presence so clear that I will not fear the dark. And tell my loved ones that I am happy.

The Resurrection Prayer of Adam

When Adam finally died I suspect his last prayer was "Lord, let me rise with my beloved Eve!" God had reached out in the beginning and touched Adam's finger and Adam had lived. God then reached out and touched Eve and she lived. Then they reached out and touched each other and discovered human love. For a while they walked in the garden hand in hand, happily unconscious of their bodies (a sure sign of perfect health). Then of course they made their great mistake in pretending to be more than they could be and became ashamed of what they were. They looked at their bodies and became ashamed and frightened. They covered their nakedness and went off to work out their salvation. They carried their love with them but now found that there was more need for caresses of consolation. Their bodies were still lovable but they became somewhat aching. They still needed a lot of love. They also needed a little liniment. Despite all their ills they were still attached to their bodies.

Death was frightening to Adam and Eve for the same reason it is to us. It seems to mark the end of the body. Adam's life began with a touch. Death came when touching was over. Adam must have wept at the prospect. I suspect that God (for old time's sake) must have hinted about the resurrection. It was the only way Adam could die happily.

Our souls are immortal but still they would weep if they could at being separated from their old buddy, the body. It is true that the poor thing gets lumpy and wrinkled, especially in our final days. It is disobedient and contrary. Despite all our commands of "Stand up straight, can't you!" it eventually bends over further and further, reaching to kiss the earth from which it came. Knowing this inevitable separation, our souls are distraught. Before he understood the message of the resurrection Adam must have perspired in fear. Though his soul was his source of life he only knew what it was to be alive through his body. He loved Eve body and soul but it was only through his body that his spirit knew of her softness, the fragrance of her hair, the laughing light of her eyes. When he held his precious Eve in close embrace, he was able to know with glee that he was not alone.

Thus it may have been, as Adam lay dying, that he voiced for the first time the prayer of a human awaiting resurrection with a beloved.

> Lord, I hope I meet Eve's soul even before the day of resurrection. Maybe we shall recognize each other (Is there some way to carry an identifying rose?) and remember. If there is some way for us to get together early, then perhaps we could search together (hand in hand or whatever is the equivalent) for those old buddies, our bodies. Then when the day of resurrection comes we won't waste any time. We can fall into each other's arms forever. When Eve and I rise up together we shall say to each other, "My, how pretty you are!" and those old buddies, our bodies, will look up to you, Lord, and blush and smile.

Jesus, how fine it was for you to save me through death and resurrection. Looking at your risen body I can believe that my body too shall rise someday. I will see you and once again enjoy the beauty of my dear, dear friends.

The Wineskin Splits

In our final days we cannot control the flow of our lives. When we were young and tired of it we knew that with patience things would change. There is no such remedy when we are very old. That's the way it shall be till the end and nothing more can be done about it. However, we can control our attitudes towards life's stages, and this is no mean power. Much of human suffering comes from attitudes towards facts rather than the facts themselves. Thus, birth can be a burden or a blessing; life, a frightening unknown or an exciting range of possibles; death, a breaking down or a breaking out. Death can be a breaking out, old wineskins finally split by the surge of our spirit reaching out for eternal life. Very literally our life ends because we split.

It all begins with the way we look at our lives. We can picture life as beginning full and ending empty. There is a peak in life which comes early on. Before we get there (as we grow up) we look forward to it, rush to reach it, finally grasp it, and spend the rest of our time trying to prevent it from slipping away. We lose this supposed fullness of youth necessarily, but for a while we pretend that we still have it. We reach a point when all pretense is impossible. We very definitely are "over the hill" and we look back with sadness and fear the future. We are convinced that the wine of life is gone and we feel cheated somehow because we are growing old. We wear out at last. We spend our final days in sadness, flat and ugly, the last precious wine pressed out of our poor old skins.

Christ sees our life quite differently. Our life is growth. Each moment is an opportunity to learn and grow in the life of God. We are constantly being filled with new life until our very existence is stretched beyond endurance. We are spaced out. We are pregnant with the growing life of God in us. The stretch lines begin to show on our poor limited skins and finally we split. The fire of life will no longer be contained. Life itself drives us toward the fire that is God and we explode!

To believe in Jesus is to believe that we are called to grow and grow through all the days of our sometimes troublesome life. We are called to grow and grow in Christ until finally with him we split the earth and fall free and unencumbered into the arms of the Father of life. Now we are no longer contained in wineskins. Our life is free to grow and grow in the house of that Father who finally and forever will "wipe away all tears from our eyes" (Rev 6:17).

> Jesus, fill me up quickly with your life so that I can get rid of this old smelly skin and put on my garment of salvation.

Day of Meeting

The day shall finally come for me to take the trip. All the baggage will have been disposed of and I will be ready to go. I wonder how it will be on that day?

Perhaps it will be like a baby going to the beach for the first time. I shall dance tentatively on the sand at first, grasping the hands of loved ones as I cautiously approach the strange rolling surf. As I get close I shall feel myself picked up and held tightly by my beloved, my arms clasped firmly around his muscled neck. He will point out my mother swimming easily in the swells and speak reassuringly about the beauty of the deepening sea.

I shall laugh, half in fear and half in anticipation, as my friend takes me deeper. I am secure in the knowledge that he has been there and back. He has already plunged through the depths and has returned for me. Now he carries me through the great adventure of my short life, entering the eternal sea in the arms of my strong, strong friend.

As we move together ever deeper into the sea I shall discover that it contains all the colors of my days. The shining silvery whiteness of my beginning is reflected in the thousand tiny mirrors of the sparkling surf. The deepening greens and blues of the surface waters remind me of my ordinary days as I sank deeper into my life, gradually becoming surrounded by the exuberantly colored flora and fauna of the sea's full life. Finally I sink into the royal purple of the deep. And then? Who knows what colors are on the other side of purple!

Some few have experienced the last fringe of this life and have returned to report a brilliant burst of light. They say it is a color unlike anything we see in the ordinary oceans of this time. But they can say no more.

My faith tells me little about that first new day. But my faith does tell me that I shall be carried there by my friend. My faith tells me that if I have reached out to him as I played and sang and danced and cried on the beach, if I have tried to search him out in the morning, noon, and dusk, then when the night and the rolling surf approaches he will lift me up. As the purpled waters race toward me he will soothe me with his words and hold me even tighter as we together go to meet the King.

My faith tells me that as the warm dark sea closes gently over me, *I shall live!* And I shall discover that my friend who holds me now at the end of my years is in fact my King: Jesus-God!

Jesus, stay close to me in the morning and in the afternoon as I build my little castles and play my little games. Stay close to me through the day so that in the evening I will be used to you and eager to reach for you as the dark surf approaches.

Also by the author:

In SEASONS OF JESUS, *published in 1978 by The Liturgical Press, Father Burt speaks from the heart as he contemplates Jesus in the gospels. Part paraphrase, part poetry, part commentary, part prayer –* SEASONS OF JESUS *is a strikingly fresh approach to the mystery of salvation by an imaginative and prayerful priest-philosopher. Meditative reading of this book is certain to lead to a larger vision and deeper appreciation of both the person and work of Jesus in our time.*